PACIFICA

BLUE PLATES

NEIL STUART

TEN SPEED PRESS
BERKELEY, CALIFORNIA

To my wife, Crystal

1☉ TEN SPEED PRESS
P.O. Box 7123
Berkeley, California 94707

FIRST PRINTING 1992

Cover and text design by Nancy Austin
Illustrations from, and after the style of artwork by Native Americans in the
    Southwest
Typesetting by Wilsted & Taylor
Photographs © 1992 by Gerry Wilson

Library of Congress Cataloging-in-Publication Data

Stuart, Neil, 1949—
    Pacifica blue plates / Neil Stuart.
        p.   cm.
    Includes index.
    ISBN 0-89815-437-5
    1. Cookery, American—California style.   2. Cafe Pacifica (San Diego, Calif.)
3. Pacifica Grill (San Diego, Calif.)   4. Pacifica Del Mar (San Diego, Calif.)
I. Title.
TX715.2.C34S78   1992
641.59794—dc20   91-12250
                                                                      CIP

Printed in the United States of America

1   2   3   4   5   -   96   95   94   93   92

ACKNOWLEDGEMENTS

Along the way, there were those who contributed their support, for which I am extremely grateful. Foremost among them are my wife, Crystal, my in-laws, Eldon and Vicky, and my parents, Sid and Lil.

My friends Frank, Lucy, Marian, Donna, and Marty were always with me in my thoughts and deserve more thanks than I can ever give.

I'd like to thank all those at the Culinary Institute of America who provided me with the fundamental knowledge that allows me to do what I do, every day, with understanding. My gratefulness extends to those restauranteurs who let me into their kitchens: Stanley Bernstein, the best employer anyone could have, who taught me, among many things, to mellow out; Richard Lavin, who opened up my exploration with food; and Barry Wine, who helped me define the limits of quality and good taste; and, above all, to Kipp Downing and Deacon Brown, who gave me their kitchen and allowed it to become my own.

The staff of Pacifica Restaurants, past and present, deserve all the gratitude I can bestow on them, especially Darrell, Scott, Bo, Bruce, Michelle, J.T., and Steve. I extend my appreciation to all the purveyors of Pacifica Grill who provide me with the ingredients and deserve much of the credit for making the food as good as it is.

The camaraderie of some of San Diego's finest chefs—Scott Meskan, Douglas Organ, and Bob Brody—provided me with both insight and moments of relaxation for which I am indebted, at least to the extent of the next round of drinks.

My thanks to Mark Miller who never fails to provide inspiration and friendship.

Special thanks to April Porro for capturing the spirit of Pacific Southwest style in her design of Pacifica Grill and to Gerry Wilson, photographer extraordinaire, who provides visions of my food to those who will not have the opportunity to come to the restaurant.

To Phil, George, Sal, Cynthia, Nancy, and the whole gang at Ten Speed Press, I want to express my gratefulness and sheer admiration for making this project a joy!

I'm also indebted to Bill Gladstone who is responsible, more than anyone, for the realization of this book.

CONTENTS

HAUTE SALSA	Fresh Tomato Salsa	2
	Avocado Salsa	2
	Chipotle Honey Salsa	3
	Mexican Beer Salsa	4
	Red Chile Paste	5
	Pineapple Salsa	6
	Red Onion and Orange Salsa	6
	Thai Marinade	7
	Teriyaki Sauce	7
	Spicy Oriental Black Bean Salsa	8
	Oriental Mustard Salsa	9
	Chinese Hot Mustard	9
	Roasted Garlic Butter	10
	Roasted Garlic Cream	11
	Maui Onion Cream	12
	Sweet Corn Cream	13
	Sweet Corn Salsa	14
	Ancho Chile Mayo	15
	Tequila and Sweet Lime Mayo	15
	Cilantro Mayo	16
	Jalapeño Honey Mustard	17
	Jalapeño Tartar Sauce	17
	Green Chile Pesto	18
	Cilantro Pesto	19
	Chinese Pesto	19

SMALL PLATES	Duck and Sun-Dried Cherry Fajita	22
	Grilled Calamari Steak with Cilantro Mayo	23
	Grilled Seafood Sausage with Roasted Garlic Butter	24
	Grilled Chicken and Cilantro Sausage with Jalapeño Honey Mustard	25
	Grilled Lamb Sausage with Charred Tomatoes and Cilantro Pesto	26
	Grilled Shrimp Cocktail with Chipotle Honey Salsa	27
	Grilled Shrimp Tacos with Radicchio and Avocado Salsa	28
	Sweetbreads with Spinach and Wild Rice Pancakes and Maui Onion Cream	29
	Kim Chee Crab Martini	30

~~~~~~

SPAGHETTI WESTERNS

LARGE PLATES

SIDEKICKS

≈≈

FINAL TEMPTATIONS

ABOUT PACIFICA
BLUE PLATES

Pacifica Blue Plates is the culmination of the six years that I served as executive chef for San Diego's foremost contemporary restaurants: Cafe Pacifica, Pacifica Grill, and Pacifica Del Mar. These dishes are also the foundation for my own restaurant, Stuart's Grill, in Del Mar, California.

The cuisine combines regional flavors in traditional and innovative ways. Time-honored recipes from Mexico, mirroring more than 400 years of culinary history, find their way onto the menu. Accents from Asia infuse the recipes with flavors that reflect San Diego's new position as the crossroads of the Pacific. And the inimitable flair and bounty of California transform food into a distinctly fresh and exciting cuisine. Spices have been tempered, techniques refined, and emphasis placed on a lighter, healthier approach to cooking. This cookbook shares the best of these creations with you.

RECIPE FOR A CHEF

I know of no family heritage or tradition that made it my destiny to become a chef. My first recollection of cooking is when I was away at college in Tallahassee, Florida, and prepared elbow macaroni and meat sauce much the way my mother had done. The second time I made it I added dried oregano. I recall thinking how much better it was and that there wasn't really much to this thing called cooking.

A few years later I cooked my first Thanksgiving dinner. I broke tradition and prepared Duck a l'Orange. Actually, I think the idea for having duck was more the result of my stove being so tiny that it couldn't accommodate a turkey than my outstanding culinary creativity.

Amidst these cooking milestones, I studied theatre in college, got a job at the telephone company in New York City, and, eventually, became a partner in a communications consulting firm. Both my partner and I had brand new sets of credit cards, which we used judiciously by dining at a different French restaurant every night. That is when I learned to eat.

After a time, I became disillusioned with the business world and moved upstate to Ithaca. The only job I could land at the time was assistant manager in a small restaurant. Each night I found myself drawn toward the kitchen, where I finally ended up working. I learned the basic principles of defrosting frozen prepared foods, making crepes, and reheating foods in a microwave. I received my first lesson on buying wines, too, when I observed the owner of the restaurant purchasing large quantities of discounted older Beaujolais only to find out later the wine was undrinkable.

A tiny bakery called Clever Hans was new in town at the time. My regular visits to buy and consume the most buttery croissants imaginable somehow got me my next job. I learned the basics of pastry work and the weekly routine of making some 500 pounds of cookies and a combined total of around 800 pounds of puff pastry, croissant, and danish dough. I also learned about quality. At this point, I became hooked and decided to attend the Culinary Institute of America in Hyde Park, New York.

Culinary school was no different than most schools. Many students, experiencing their first taste of living away from home, spent more time finding out how to get out of a stew than learning what it takes to prepare one. As an older student, I managed to keep focused on learning the art of cooking and graduated first in my class, not as a chef, but as a novice, trained in the basics, about to enter the real world of cooking. I was given some sound advice by one of my instructors who directed me to work in as many restaurants as possible to make up in experience for the time I couldn't regain from my "misspent" youth.

Following this course, I worked in New York at the Atrium Club, Vista International Hotel, and then, drawn by the chance to be part of the opening of a new restaurant, I took my first chef's position at the 23rd Street Bar and Grill. Here, along with the assistance of the owner, Stanley Bernstein, I created my first menu. Composed of the likes of Roast Chicken, Liver and Onions, Burgers, and Chili, it didn't seem like much, but Stanley allowed me the opportunity to learn the business aspects of running a kitchen. This involved ordering, scheduling, costing, and learning to supervise people.

My next stop was Lavin's Restaurant. Richard Lavin had turned the old Engineer's Club in midtown Manhattan into one of the first restaurants that was an advocate for the New American Cuisine. I was hired as the dinner chef and couldn't have been more excited. The menu, a melting pot of cuisines, permitted me to blend styles and flavors into something new. Richard loved to taste the new creations, and I can still see him smiling and proclaiming, "something wonderful is happening in my mouth!" while he tasted a new dish.

While Lavin's provided me with a venue for exploration, I yearned to learn those differences that set a restaurant far above the rest. One day I picked up the phone, called Barry Wine, chef-owner of the Quilted Giraffe, and asked for a job. That was simple enough, but Barry explained to me that the rest of the hiring process wasn't as easy. It required a tryout, both for me to determine if I really wanted to work there and, of course, if they wanted me. I agreed to come in and within hours headed for my tryout at one of the most highly rated restaurants in this country. In 1983, I still wasn't all that sure of myself and didn't know whether I would pass the tryout. What I did know was that as long as I was there, even if only for a matter of hours, I was going to find out their secrets. I examined everything that went on, hardly saying a word, until they finally asked me if I wanted to work there.

The "secrets" I soon learned at the Quilted Giraffe seem surprisingly simple. Use only the freshest and best quality ingredients available, prepare them in a manner that highlights their natural flavors, and be sure to cook them properly.

During this period of time I took my first trip to France to taste firsthand the food that dreams are supposed to be made of. At the Hotel Grand Ecuyer, tucked away in the small village of Cordes, I had the best meal of my life (thus far) cooked by Chef Yves Thuries. During my travels in France, I never experienced one bad meal, but I came to realize that some of the food we had in the States was as good, if not better, than what I had been sampling.

Soon after returning from my trip, lottery fever was rampant in New York City as the pot swelled to one of the largest ever. People fantasized how life would change upon winning; when asked by my wife, Crystal, what I would do if I won, I responded that we would pick ourselves up and move to a more desirable city and each pursue our chosen career. Crystal observed that we didn't need to win the lottery to do that. We moved to San Diego a month later.

I began working at Pacifica Grill in 1985, two months short of its first year anniversary. Owners Kipp Downing and Deacon Brown presided over an eclectic menu, similar in style to the foods I cooked while at Lavin's. Although patrons enjoyed the menu overall, they were not as comfortable with it as could be hoped for. I was perplexed as to what to do.

I had been observing the exciting culinary changes taking place across America. Larry Forgione recaptured an American identity and was defining its future course at the River Cafe in Brooklyn. In Berkeley, California, at Chez Panisse, Alice Waters was teaching honesty and purity of ingredients and was nurturing a remarkable number of America's best chefs. Not least among those who worked with Waters are Jeremiah Tower, who demonstrates with great finesse the new direction of American cooking at Stars in San Francisco, and Mark Miller, now at Coyote Cafe in Santa Fe, who teaches us to cook with chiles and more chiles. The common thread between these individuals' cooking was that each had a regional identity and used only the freshest local ingredients available. It made sense.

Little by little, I began to add dishes to the menu that reflected San Diego. By combining the traditions and robust flavors of Mexico with the flair and bounty of southern California, I created food that people in San Diego could relate to and a style that was becoming my own. It was during this time that my skills as a chef matured. I was confident in the things I could and couldn't do and was able to practice my craft without encumbrances. Two years after this transition began, I defined the style as Pacific Southwest cuisine.

USER'S GUIDE

My goal while writing *Pacifica Blue Plates* was to make it a useful source for creative home cooking. And while you needn't be a gourmet cook to follow my recipes, this is not a kitchen primer for beginning cooks. Therefore, I've not included certain basic recipes such as chicken stock and mayonnaise that can be found in any number of cookbooks.

I realize there's more to cooking than just following recipes, which are only guides for both the inexperienced and veteran cook. When all your skills, your common sense, and your sense of taste, smell, and sight are not enough, try following the instructions! My recipes rely on quality ingredients and proper execution. Most of the preparations are simple, but to help you get started, on the following pages I've listed a few simple guidelines and explained those procedures, fundamental to the recipes I've created, with which you may be unfamiliar. The recipes using these techniques are cross-referenced to the How To pages in this User's Guide. I hope they'll save you some time and frustration, as well as from any unexpected last-minute dinners at your local fast-food heaven.

I've also compiled a list of ingredients called for in this cookbook that might be difficult to obtain or with which you may be unacquainted. I've provided definitions, hints on where you might find these special ingredients, and possible substitutions.

MENU PLANNING

Menus should be balanced, not just in a nutritional sense, but in a variety of ways. If you plan to serve a course that's heavy, make sure the other courses are light. Use contrasting flavors, textures, and colors to create interest. Don't select overly complicated dishes for every course. If you choose one recipe that's difficult, make sure the others are easy. If possible, concoct a menu that allows you to prepare most of the ingredients or recipes in advance so when it comes time to serve, you can enjoy the moment with your guests.

SHOPPING FOR INGREDIENTS

Markets contain many more items than we realize. Most often we're so preoccupied with the specific ingredients we came to purchase that we don't see all the others available. Every now and then, rather than following your habitual shopping patterns, walk through your market, aisle by aisle, to see what they really offer. You'll be amazed to discover many of those gourmet ingredients that you thought were impossible to find right there on the shelf.

Chefs know that the meals they prepare depend on the quality of ingredients they purchase. Learn to rely on your butcher and produce manager to help you obtain the best products available. In time, their knowledge will become yours.

ORGANIZE THYSELF!

I stress nothing more strongly than organization in the art of cooking. Do what you can ahead of time. Measure, clean, peel, seed, chop, cut, and then, and only then, begin cooking.

HOW TO:

Toast Nuts and Croutons

Place nuts or croutons on a baking pan in a preheated 350-degree oven and bake, stirring every three to four minutes, until they take on a light golden brown color, approximately twelve to eighteen minutes for croutons and twelve to fifteen minutes for nuts.

Peel Tomatoes

With the tip of a sharp knife, remove the tomatoes' stems. Score the opposite ends of the tomatoes with an X and plunge into boiling water for twenty to thirty seconds. Remove the tomatoes and immerse in cold water until they are cool enough to handle. When cool, the skin should pull away easily.

Place whole peppers on a baking pan in a preheated 350-degree oven and roast until skins are charred lightly. Remove peppers from oven and allow them to cool. If desired, when cool enough to handle, peppers can be skinned by simply pulling the skin away.

Roast Peppers

Remove seeds by cutting peppers or chiles open and gently scraping seeds away with the edge of a knife. When seeding any of the spicy varieties kitchen gloves should be worn to avoid direct contact with the hands.

Seed Peppers and Chiles

Scrape the mussel shells with a knife, pull off the beards, rinse in cold water, and place in cold, salted water for one hour to remove any excess sand. Rinse again in cold water and use as desired.

Clean Mussels

Simply pull the shell away from the meat of the shrimp, retaining the tail piece if desired. With a small sharp knife, cut an incision one-eighth inch deep along the entire back of the shrimp to the beginning of the tail. This will reveal the long, thin intestinal tract that can be removed by simply brushing it away with the edge of a paper towel. Rinse the shrimp under cold water and use as desired.

Peel and Devein Shrimp

Grab the head and tentacles with one hand and with your other hand pull on the body, breaking it away from the head. Cut the tentacles from the head with a sharp knife and discard the head. Tentacles are now ready for use. Peel the grayish skin off the body and discard. Inside the body is transparent cartilage that should also be disposed of. Wash body thoroughly under cold water, remove the two flaps and discard, and cut the body into rings.

Clean Calamari

Clean soft-shell crabs by lifting up the side flaps underneath the body and removing the featherlike gills and the flap underneath. Rinse under cold water and use as directed.

Clean Soft-Shell Crabs

BASIC INGREDIENTS

In all cases where butter is called for, use unsalted butter. Using unsalted butter gives you more control over the flavor of the final product. While you may substitute margarine or oil for some dishes, do not make substitutions for butter in butter sauces, such

Butter

as the Wild Mushroom and Ginger Butter and Roasted Garlic Butter, or in any of the desserts.

Chicken Stock   Where chicken stock is specified, it refers to homemade, unsalted stock. You may use any of the canned varieties available, but they usually contain salt and you should adjust the recipe accordingly.

Cream   Whipping cream and heavy cream are, essentially, the same. You can substitute half-and-half in soups and sauces calling for cream but that will diminish their richness and thickening ability.

Herbs   Many chefs say that fresh herbs are always superior to dried. I contend it's a matter of how they're used. In each recipe, I specify fresh or dried, and substitutions cannot be made without affecting the outcome of the recipe.

Pepper   I love freshly ground black pepper. It's certainly more robust than preground varieties and more distinctive than white pepper. Freshly ground black pepper was one of the "secrets" I learned while working at the Quilted Giraffe.

Salt   In every recipe, I specify coarse salt. This refers to both sea salt and kosher salt. If you are still using pouring salt for seasoning, change your ways. This is, definitely, one of those "chef's secrets" that you need to adopt. Do a taste comparison and see for yourself what a difference in flavor it makes.

NOT-SO-BASIC INGREDIENTS

Achiote Paste   This Yucatan seasoning paste is made from ground annatto seeds, garlic, and other herbs and spices. Most often with the Mexican speciality pork pibil, it is the basis of Yucatan barbeque. You find achiote paste mostly in Hispanic markets.

Anaheim Chiles   Depending on their place of origin, these long, narrow, green chiles range from mild to hot. Fresh Anaheim chiles are relatively common in markets, but if unavailable, the canned variety, found in most stores along with other Mexican foods, can be substituted.

Ancho Chiles   Dried version of the poblano chile, these dark red pods produce a deep, rich flavor with varying degrees of heat. Available in most large markets and Hispanic specialty markets, substitute pasilla chiles if unavailable.

This aged red wine vinegar, usually of Italian origin, has a wonderful rich flavor. Available in Italian specialty markets, as well as most major markets, but if it can't be obtained substitute a good red wine vinegar.

Balsamic Vinegar

Used as a wrapping to bake and steam foods, banana leaves impart a unique flavor to dishes. If you don't have access to a banana tree, you can find banana leaves in the frozen food department of Oriental and Hispanic food stores in your area. Otherwise you may use parchment paper or tinfoil instead.

Banana Leaves

Water buffalo milk cheese, usually imported from Italy, is extremely smooth and creamy compared to the commercial varieties of mozzarella. Many Italian markets sell freshly made mozzarella that, although not made from buffalo's milk, is very good.

Buffalo Mozzarella

Due to the increasing popularity of Caribbean cooking, this fiery blend of spices from the Islands is making its way to the spice and gourmet departments of many specialty and major market chains.

Caribbean Jerk Spice

An Asian concoction of red chiles and garlic, this is a source of *hot* for those so inclined. Look for it along with other Oriental foods in most stores and in the condiment section of Oriental markets. You may substitute your favorite hot sauce, but those containing a large proportion of vinegar will produce adverse effects on recipes calling for chile and garlic paste.

Chile and Garlic Paste

A blend of dried cinnamon, anise, cloves, fennel, and Szechuan pepper, Chinese five spice is widely available in Oriental food sections and specialty stores.

Chinese Five Spice

Made from yellow plums, this Oriental condiment is for everything from eggrolls to roast duck and is available in most stores.

Chinese Plum Sauce

The chipotle is a dried and smoked jalapeño pepper. I find that the canned variety, sometimes labeled "en adobo," works best. Available in Hispanic specialty stores.

Chipotle Chiles

Also known as Chinese parsley and coriander, this peppery herb has predominance in many Mexican and Asian dishes. I've found

Cilantro

cilantro to be an herb that people have definite opinions on, they either strongly like or dislike it. Don't substitute the dried variety. For a different twist, try using watercress if you can't find cilantro in your market next to the parsley and other fresh herbs.

Coconut Milk Usually a canned product, the milk you purchase should be unsweetened. Found in most Oriental food sections and markets.

Daikon This delicately flavored white Chinese radish looks a bit like a giant albino carrot. Daikon is often used as a garnish for sushi. If not available in your produce store, substitute mild radishes.

Dumpling, Eggroll, and Wonton Skins These fresh pastry doughs are widely available in major supermarkets and Oriental specialty stores. I've found them in the produce section, the refrigerated food section, and even in the frozen food section. Each type is different enough from the others that you won't want to make substitutions.

Eggroll Skins *See* Dumpling, Eggroll, and Wonton Skins

Epazote Also called wormseed, this Mexican herb has a somewhat peppery flavor with a mint aftertaste and is most often used in conjunction with bean dishes. It is said to reduce beans' gaseous quality. If only dried epazote is available, substitute half the quantity of fresh called for in the recipe. If unavailable in any form, use cilantro in its place.

Habañero Chile Sauce The habañero chile is one of the hottest in the Americas. It has a deep, meaty flavor, and although very hot, the heat doesn't linger too long. A number of different brands of habañero chile sauces are available in condiment sections of many supermarkets. If unavailable in your area, substitute your favorite hot sauce.

Hoisin Sauce A Chinese barbeque sauce made from soybeans, vinegar, and spices, hoisin sauce is a basic in all food markets with Asian sections.

Jalapeño Peppers This small, hot green chile, if not available fresh, can usually be found canned alongside other Mexican foods. Serrano chiles make a good substitute.

Similar in flavor to water chestnuts, jicama is a large, white root vegetable with light brown skin that needs to be peeled before using. **Jicama**

Used in the preparation of Korean Kim Chee (pickled cabbage), this vinegar and red chile marinade can be found most easily in Oriental markets. **Kim Chee Marinade**

Lemon grass, a stalk with a mellow lemon flavor, is used mostly in Asia to accent soups, stews, and sauces and in Mexico to make iced tea. Oriental markets are your best bet when looking for lemon grass. It is generally available dried, too. Although it won't approximate the true flavor, you can use the zest of fresh lemons as a substitute. **Lemon Grass**

Mirin is Japanese sweet rice wine, used for cooking, and can be found in most Oriental food sections and specialty stores. **Mirin**

Soybeans preserved in salt with ginger and garlic, these beans are the primary ingredient in Oriental black bean sauces. They must be soaked for half an hour and rinsed well before using. You will find them in Oriental food markets. **Oriental Fermented Black Beans**

Coarse Japanese bread crumbs, panko can be found in most Oriental food sections and specialty stores. **Panko Bread Crumbs**

This Jamaican condiment, made from tomatoes, mangoes, tamarind, vinegar, and a variety of spices, can be found in most markets alongside the ketchup bottles and jars of steak sauces. **Pickapepper Sauce**

Puff pastry, a bastion of French pastry making, is the shell from which napoleons are made. You can usually find boxes of frozen puff pastry sheets in the market where frozen pie shells are located. Another source is your local bakery, which might be willing to sell you fresh sheets. **Puff Pastry**

This ruby red member of the chicory family is a crisp, slightly bitter lettuce that accompanies other salad greens wonderfully. **Radicchio**

Oriental vinegar made from rice comes both seasoned and unseasoned. If your market carries both varieties, select the seasoned vinegar. **Rice Wine Vinegar**

Rose's Lime Juice	Find this sweetened lime juice where nonalcoholic mixes for mixed drinks for sold.
Smoked Salmon Jerky	Not an easy product to find, this jerky is made with smoked salmon. Your best chance to acquire it locally will be in gourmet markets.
Soba Noodles	These thin, dried noodles are made from buckwheat flour. Very delicate in flavor, soba noodles can be found in Oriental food sections and markets, as well as health food stores. If you must substitute, use angel hair pasta.
Star Anise	This seedpod, shaped like an eight-point star, produces a rich licorice flavor. Star anise is available in Oriental markets where other dried spices and herbs are located. Fennel seeds can be used as a substitute.
Sun-Dried Tomatoes	You can usually find these intensely flavored tomatoes dry packed, in which case they must be reconstituted briefly in hot water before using, or packed in oil. Unless I want to use the oil for a specific purpose, I prefer the dry-packed tomatoes. Find them in some supermarkets, most gourmet stores, and Italian markets.
Sun-Dried Cherries	Like raisins, these cherries are intense in flavor. Look for them in gourmet and health food stores.
Sweet Red Bean Paste	Most readily found in Oriental markets in the canned food section, this sweet bean product is often used in desserts.
Szechuan Peppercorns	A small seed similar in appearance to a black peppercorn, but with more aromatic qualities than spiciness, it is readily available in Oriental food sections and markets.
Tamarind Paste	Tamarind is a tart, tropical fruit found in Mexican, Asian, and East Indian cooking. The paste is obtained by boiling tamarind pods and scraping out the pulp that results from the seeds. Found most frequently in Oriental and East Indian specialty food stores.
Tomatillos	These husk-covered tart green tomatoes can be found fresh or canned (by other Mexican products) in many markets. Do not confuse them with unripe red tomatoes.

The green powder, Japanese dried horseradish, is moistened with water to create a very pungent paste, served traditionally with sashimi and sushi. Small cans of it can be purchased in Oriental food sections and markets.

Wasabi Powder

See Dumpling, Eggroll, and Wonton Skins

Wonton Skins

HAUTE SALSA

When I arrived in San Diego from New York City, I was armed with a chef's usual repertoire of sauces, relishes, chutneys, and vinaigrette dressings. My very first menus at Pacifica Grill contained items that were described as accompanied by the likes of "Cranberry Chutney," "Green Peppercorn Relish," and "Wild Mushroom Vinaigrette." I was sure that the sauces would elicit a positive response if I could get anyone to taste the dishes. Day after day they remained unordered.

Confused, even depressed, I approached the topic of my "no sell sauces" with my sous-chef, Darrell, one of the few natives of southern California. His reply was simple. "People in San Diego just can't relate to those terms. What they *do* understand is *salsa*."

There's something about the world "salsa" that evokes more than "sauce," its literal translation. Spicy and rhythmic, salsa has that certain pizzazz! Whatever it is, if I hadn't used the term, my dishes never would have received the acceptance they have, and I would not have written this cookbook.

FRESH TOMATO SALSA

2 cups tomatoes, diced
½ cup tomatillos, diced
½ cup red onion, diced
1 clove garlic, minced
1 small jalapeño pepper, seeded and minced
    (see directions on page xix)
½ cup cilantro, chopped
1 tablespoon fresh lime juice
¼ cup rice wine vinegar
1 teaspoon sugar
1 teaspoon coarse salt
⅛ teaspoon freshly ground black pepper

Mix all ingredients in a bowl. Allow salsa to set 1 hour before serving so flavors develop. Serve at room temperature.

MAKES 3 CUPS

There's just no reason to eat store-bought tomato salsa anymore! Whether you call this "salsa cruda," "salsa fresca," or whatever, when you use vine ripe tomatoes and serve it with a basket of fresh, hot tortillas, nothing comes close to being this good. You can spice the recipe up, or down. If you can't find tomatillos, which are those small, tart green tomatoes, you can eliminate them from the recipe.

AVOCADO SALSA

2 medium avocados, peeled, seeded, and diced
½ cup tomatoes, seeded and diced
¼ cup cilantro, chopped
3 tablespoons red onion, diced
1 clove garlic, minced
1 tablespoon fresh lime juice
½ teaspoon jalapeño pepper, seeded and minced
    (see directions on page xix)
1 teaspoon coarse salt
⅛ teaspoon freshly ground black pepper

Combine and gently mix all ingredients in a bowl. Salsa is best when used the same day it is prepared.

MAKES 3 CUPS

Avocado is one of the many fruits native to South America that was exported to France and put on a culinary pedestal before becoming popular here in the United States.

This version of guacamole, in which the avocado is diced instead of smashed as in the typical recipe, takes on a whole new character and the individual flavors remain more distinct. Liven up this salsa by adding more jalapeños, or make it more refreshing with another squeeze of lime.

CHIPOTLE HONEY SALSA

1 can (3½ ounces) pickled chipotle
½ cup water
1 can (6 ounces) tomato paste
⅔ cup honey
1 bunch cilantro, chopped
1 tablespoon fresh lime juice

Combine all ingredients in a blender or food processor and blend until smooth. Serve chilled. Keeps refrigerated for 1 week.

MAKES 2½ CUPS

Short of food to distribute at a cooking demonstration I was giving, I improvised this salsa with the hope that if it was hot enough, I'd have plenty of food to go around. I quickly threw together a number of ingredients, including the fiery chipotle chile, and my kitchen staff agreed that I had finally gone beyond the limit. Just what I had hoped for!

Of course, when everyone at the demonstration loved the salsa and hollered for more, all I could do was go back to my kitchen and recreate this recipe. It's become an all-time favorite and my nomination to replace old-fashioned cocktail sauce. Use this salsa to spice up burgers, steak, and almost any food on which you might normally use ketchup.

MEXICAN BEER SALSA

This is my adaptation of a regional Mexican recipe. I use this salsa as my all-purpose tomato sauce. The flavor varies a great deal depending on the beer you select. I prefer a darker beer like Bohemia. Try a different brand each time until you achieve the flavor you like best.

4 dried ancho chiles
6 large ripe tomatoes
¾ cup white onion, diced
4 cloves garlic
1 tablespoon coarse salt
½ teaspoon freshly ground black pepper
½ cup Mexican beer

Preheat oven to 400 degrees. Soak ancho chiles in hot water until soft, about 10–15 minutes. Drain water and stem and seed the chiles (see directions on page xix).

Place tomatoes, onion, and garlic in a small roasting pan; put in oven for 15–20 minutes, until the skins of the tomatoes begin to char. Remove from oven and place tomato mixture and the ancho chiles in a blender or food processor and pulse briefly, allowing the salsa to remain somewhat chunky.

Turn salsa into a small saucepan and bring mixture to a simmer; then, stir in the salt, pepper, and beer. Remove from heat. Salsa should be served warm.

MAKES 4 CUPS

RED CHILE PASTE

8 cloves garlic
10 dried ancho chiles
¼ cup sherry wine vinegar
½ teaspoon ground cinnamon
¼ teaspoon ground cumin
½ teaspoon dried thyme
½ teaspoon dried oregano
½ teaspoon freshly ground black pepper
1 teaspoon coarse salt

Preheat oven to 350 degrees. Place garlic cloves in a pan and roast to a golden brown, approximately 12–15 minutes. Cover chiles with warm water and soak for about 10 minutes, until softened. Drain water and remove seeds and stems (see directions on page xix).

In a blender or food processor, combine the garlic and chiles with the remaining ingredients and process into a smooth paste. Refrigerated, paste will keep for 2–3 weeks.

MAKES 1 CUP

This is a Mexican *adobo* paste, used traditionally as a marinade for meats and in the preparation of various stews. I also use it as a flavoring agent for Ancho Chile Mayo and Ancho Honey Glaze (recipes on pages 15 and 124).

PINEAPPLE SALSA

Fruit gives new meaning to salsa. Simultaneously sweet and spicy, this pineapple salsa fits in with today's lighter approach to dining. For something even more unusual, try adding a touch of dark rum.

1 1/2 cups fresh pineapple, diced
1 small jalapeño pepper, seeded and minced
    (see directions on page xix)
1 medium red bell pepper, seeded and diced
1/2 cup cilantro, chopped
1 tablespoon fresh lime juice
1 teaspoon honey

Place the ingredients in a small bowl and mix until combined. Serve at room temperature.

MAKES 2 CUPS

RED ONION AND ORANGE SALSA

This recipe was created to complement one of our signature dishes, Canarditas (recipe on page 111). Although its origins are classical, the salsa is modern and refreshing, and perfect with duckling.

4 large oranges
1/2 cup red onion, halved and sliced thinly
1/2 cup cilantro, chopped
1/8 teaspoon freshly ground black pepper

Carefully, peel, seed, and separate the oranges into segments. Any excess juice should be collected in a bowl with the oranges. Gently mix the onion and cilantro with the fruit; season with pepper. Serve at room temperature. Salsa is best when used the same day it is prepared.

MAKES 3 CUPS

Kim Chee Crab Martini (page 30) ⇒

THAI MARINADE

2 cups Teriyaki Sauce
1/4 cup fresh ginger, minced
1/4 cup tamarind paste
1/2 cup chile and garlic paste

Combine all ingredients in a small saucepan and bring the mixture to a simmer over low heat. Stir well to ensure that the tamarind paste is dissolved, remove from heat, and allow to cool to room temperature before using.

MAKES 3 CUPS

Thai marinades and sauces are wonderfully complex. I've simplified the preparation but not the flavors of this marinade. It's spicy, so use with caution or modify the recipe by reducing the amount of chile and garlic paste. This marinade also works great as a baste for grilled chicken, meats, and seafood and keeps well refrigerated so you'll want to make the full recipe.

TERIYAKI SAUCE

1 tablespoon sesame seeds, toasted
        (see directions on page xviii)
1 cup soy sauce
1 1/2 teaspoons sesame oil
1/2 cup sugar
2 cloves garlic, minced
2 teaspoons fresh ginger, minced
1 cup scallions, sliced thinly

Place all ingredients in a small saucepan over moderate heat. Bring to a boil to allow the sugar to dissolve. Remove from heat and cool before using.

MAKES 1 1/4 CUPS

There's a wide assortment of bottled teriyaki sauces to choose from on supermarket shelves. But this recipe is so simple and so good, why not make it yourself? You'll find this sauce is used in many of the recipes in this book. Refrigerated, it keeps well for 6–8 weeks.

SPICY ORIENTAL
BLACK BEAN SALSA

Oriental black bean sauces vary as much as barbeque sauces, each with its own nuances and dedicated fans. I had a difficult time trying to re-create individual sauces until I decided to simply "borrow" the best of each to form my own unique variation. The lemon grass is important; its mellow flavor more far-reaching than lemon zest or juice. If you can't find fresh lemon grass, go ahead and sub-stitute a quarter cup fresh lemon juice and one teaspoon lemon zest. We serve this with our Wok-Charred Catfish (rec-ipe on page 89), but if you love spice, you'll find countless ways to use this salsa.

¼ cup Oriental fermented black beans
2 tablespoons peanut oil
4 cloves garlic, minced
1 teaspoon fresh ginger, minced
¼ cup scallions, sliced thinly
¼ cup red bell pepper, diced
¾ cup Teriyaki Sauce (page 7)
½ cup chicken stock
½ stalk fresh lemon grass
1½ teaspoons chile and garlic paste
¼ teaspoon Szechuan peppercorns, crushed
2 tablespoons cornstarch
¼ cup water
1½ teaspoons sesame oil

Rinse black beans under cold running water for 10 minutes to remove some of the saltiness. Squeeze dry and chop coarsely.

Heat peanut oil in a saucepan over moderate heat and add the garlic, ginger, scallions, and red bell pepper. Stirring, cook for 2 minutes and then add the Teriyaki Sauce, chicken stock, lemon grass, black beans, chile and garlic paste, and Szechuan pepper-corns. Bring to a boil and allow to simmer for 10 minutes.

Remove the lemon grass. Dissolve cornstarch in the cold water and stir into the sauce to thicken. When sauce returns to a boil, remove from heat and stir in sesame oil. Serve warm.

MAKES 2 CUPS

ORIENTAL MUSTARD SALSA

2 tablespoons sweet butter
4 cloves garlic, minced
3 cups fresh shiitake mushrooms, sliced
1/4 cup Teriyaki Sauce (page 7)
1/2 cup heavy cream
1 cup chicken stock
1/4 cup grain mustard
1 tablespoon fresh lemon juice
1 pinch freshly ground black pepper

In a small saucepan, melt butter over moderate heat and cook garlic and mushrooms until tender. Add the Teriyaki Sauce, cream, and chicken stock; bring to a boil. Simmer gently until volume is reduced by one-fourth. Remove from heat and stir in mustard, lemon juice, and black pepper. Serve warm.

MAKES 2 CUPS

There's nothing authentic about this sauce, but it goes great with my Chinese Chicken Ravioli (recipe on page 76). This salsa is so rich and appealing you will want to make extra for leftovers.

CHINESE HOT MUSTARD

1/4 cup Colman's Mustard
1/4 cup sugar
2–3 tablespoons warm tap water

In a bowl, mix the mustard powder and sugar together. Slowly whisk in the warm water until mixture has the consistency of thickened cream. Refrigerated, mustard will keep for 2–3 days. Bring to room temperature before serving. If mixture thickens, thin with a little warm water.

MAKES 1/2 CUP

If there was one thing I learned while working at the Quilted Giraffe in New York City, it was that simple food can be spectacular when impeccable ingredients and precise execution are combined. You can't get much simpler than this hot mustard. At the Quilted, we served it on lamb racks, and at Pacifica Del Mar, on Sugar-Spiced Barbequed King Salmon (see recipe on page 91). Don't hesitate to use it on your favorite eggroll!

ROASTED GARLIC BUTTER

This is no ordinary garlic butter. Use it to complement most seafood, particularly grilled shrimp and lobster. It's spectacular as a dipping sauce for steamed clams. You can even serve it tossed with fresh pasta!

8 cloves garlic
2 cloves shallot, minced
2 teaspoons fresh lime juice
2 tablespoons white wine
1 cup (2 sticks) sweet butter, cold
1 teaspoon coarse salt
¼ teaspoon freshly ground black pepper

Preheat oven to 350 degrees. Place garlic cloves on a pan and roast 15–20 minutes until garlic is golden brown. Remove from oven and allow to cool. When cool, mash garlic with the back of a spoon until a smooth paste is achieved.

In a small saucepan over moderate heat, combine shallot with the lime juice and white wine and cook until almost all the liquid has evaporated. Lower heat, add garlic paste, and, while whisking constantly, add the butter in 2 or 3 pieces. When butter is totally incorporated, remove from the heat, season with salt and pepper to serve. This sauce does not reheat well, so enjoy it to the last drop!

MAKES 1¼ CUPS

ROASTED GARLIC CREAM

12 cloves garlic
2 tablespoons sweet butter
2 large shallots, minced
1½ cups chicken stock
3 cups heavy cream
1 tablespoon coarse salt
¼ teaspoon freshly ground black pepper
1 teaspoon fresh lime juice

Preheat oven to 350 degrees. Place garlic cloves on a pan and roast approximately 15–20 minutes, until cloves are a rich golden brown. Remove from the oven to cool. When garlic has cooled, place in a food processor or blender and purée into a smooth paste.

In a saucepan over moderate heat, melt the butter, adding the shallots and cooking until translucent. Add the chicken stock and reduce liquid by half. Add cream and roasted garlic paste and, again, reduce liquid by half. Season with salt, pepper, and lime juice and serve.

MAKES 2 CUPS

The virtues of garlic are outweighed only by those of roasted garlic. Roasting mellows garlic into sweet, nutty flavors. Roasted Garlic Cream is featured with our Crab Enchiladas (recipe on page 50). It's also wonderful with roast turkey and mashed potatoes! If you become addicted to roasted garlic like I have, you'll want to roast up a huge batch, purée it, and keep it around to use in everything from tomato sauce to mayonnaise.

MAUI ONION CREAM

If it weren't for this recipe and Roasted Garlic Cream (recipe on page 11), I could easily eliminate cream from my menus and my diet. When something is this good, you should start your diet tomorrow. If you can't get Maui onions, other varieties like Vidalia and Chilean can be substituted successfully. If you can't find any of these sweet onions, go ahead and start your diet today.

This sauce accompanies our grilled Sweetbreads (recipe on page 29). Try thinning with chicken stock and serve the sauce as soup, topped with toasted croutons.

2 tablespoons sweet butter
2 cloves garlic, minced
2 cups Maui onion, halved and sliced
¼ cup Riesling wine
1 cup chicken stock
3 cups heavy cream
1 tablespoon coarse salt
¼ teaspoon freshly ground black pepper
1 teaspoon fresh lemon juice

Melt the butter in a saucepan over moderate heat; add the garlic and onion and cook until they're translucent. Add the wine and continue cooking until almost all of it has evaporated. Pour in the chicken stock and reduce liquid by half. Add heavy cream and reduce liquid again by half. Season with salt, pepper, and lemon juice and serve.

MAKES 2 CUPS

SWEET CORN CREAM

1½ cups fresh corn kernels
2 cups heavy cream
2 cloves garlic
1 tablespoon sugar
1 teaspoon coarse salt
¼ teaspoon freshly ground black pepper

There aren't too many foods that I would refrain from serving with this sauce. I'd even consider calling it a soup and serving the cream by itself.

Remove raw kernels from corn cobs with a sharp knife. Combine the corn, cream, garlic, and sugar in a small saucepan and bring mixture to a boil over moderate heat. Reduce heat and simmer for 10 minutes.

Place ingredients in a blender or food processor and purée until smooth. Run cream through a fine strainer to remove all the corn solids. Return mixture to stove to reheat, season with salt and pepper, and serve.

MAKES 2 CUPS

SWEET CORN SALSA

Corn has universal appeal in this country. I feel blessed that I can get it fresh year-round and offer it in this buttery fashion with grilled chicken. This salsa does justice to lobster, too.

2 cups fresh corn kernels
3 tablespoons sweet butter, cold, cut into pieces
¼ cup tomatoes, seeded and diced
1 small jalapeño pepper, seeded and minced
    (see directions on page xix)
2 tablespoons red onion, minced
2 tablespoons cilantro, chopped
¼ cup rice wine vinegar
⅛ teaspoon freshly ground black pepper
¼ teaspoon coarse salt

Cut raw kernels off cobs with a sharp knife. Combine all ingredients in a saucepan over high heat and stir while bringing salsa to a boil. When butter has melted completely and takes on the look of a light butter sauce, remove from heat and serve immediately.

MAKES 3 CUPS

ANCHO CHILE MAYO

1 cup mayonnaise
2 tablespoons Red Chile Paste (page 5)
1 tablespoon cilantro, chopped
1 teaspoon fresh lime juice

Combine ingredients in a small bowl and mix until integrated. Refrigerated, keeps 2–3 weeks. This mayonnaise turns cold chicken or turkey sandwiches into a real treat.

MAKES 1¼ CUPS

TEQUILA AND SWEET LIME MAYO

1 cup mayonnaise
2 tablespoons pine nuts, toasted and chopped
    (see directions on page xviii)
2 teaspoons tequila
4 teaspoons Rose's Lime Juice
1 tablespoon parsley, chopped
1 pinch freshly ground black pepper

Combine all ingredients in a small bowl and mix until combined.

This mayonnaise is excellent for chicken or shrimp salad sandwiches and, refrigerated, keeps well for 2–3 weeks.

MAKES 1¼ CUPS

MAYONNAISE

Whether you buy it or make it from scratch, mayonnaise needn't be plain. You can add almost anything that suits your taste, changing this simple condiment into something dramatic. The following recipes demonstrate just a few of the flavor creations possible. If you're watching your fat intake, these recipes work well using low-fat mayonnaise.

CILANTRO MAYO

3 large eggs
1 teaspoon dry mustard
2 bunches cilantro, chopped
¼ cup rice wine vinegar
1 clove garlic, minced
¼ teaspoon freshly ground black pepper
1 teaspoon coarse salt
1 cup peanut oil

Combine all ingredients except the peanut oil in a blender or food processor. Begin to process and add the oil in a steady stream until completely incorporated.

You'll want to try this dressing as a dipping sauce for grilled seafood! Refrigerated, keeps 2–3 weeks.

MAKES 2 CUPS

JALAPEÑO HONEY MUSTARD

½ cup Dijon mustard
½ cup honey
1 tablespoon pickled jalapeño pepper, seeded
    and minced (see directions on page xix)
1 tablespoon juice from pickled jalapeño pepper

In a bowl, mix all ingredients until combined.

MAKES 1 CUP

Much like mayonnaise, you can do almost anything with mustard. Although I love all varieties, I've found Dijon mustard to be the best vehicle for journeys into new flavors. Use this spicy mustard as a glaze for chicken or ham or as a dipping sauce for raw vegetables.

JALAPEÑO TARTAR SAUCE

1 cup mayonnaise
1 tablespoon dill pickle relish
2 tablespoons pickled jalapeño pepper, seeded
    and diced (see directions on page xix)
1 tablespoon scallions, sliced thinly
1 tablespoon mustard
½ teaspoon fresh lemon juice
⅛ teaspoon freshly ground black pepper

Mix all ingredients in a bowl until combined.

MAKES 1¼ CUPS

The peppers in this tartar sauce add spice to one of our most often requested preparations, Mustard Catfish (recipe on page 88). If you love jalapeño peppers, you'll want to enjoy this sauce for all your seafood dishes on which you normally use tartar sauce.

GREEN CHILE PESTO

Invariably, in the past pesto referred to the Italian concoction of fresh basil, garlic, pine nuts, and cheese. Or so it seemed. Nowadays, you can find any number of pestos that, other than concentrating flavor—whatever it might be, bear no resemblance to the traditional. Use pesto to complement the flavors of chicken, steak, and pasta.

6 medium Anaheim chiles, seeded and chopped roughly (see directions on page xix)
3 cloves garlic
½ cup cilantro, chopped
½ cup pine nuts, toasted (see directions on page xviii)
2 tablespoons fresh lime juice
1 teaspoon jalapeño pepper, seeded and minced (see directions on page xix)
1 tablespoon coarse salt
¼ peanut oil
1 cup freshly grated Parmesan cheese

Combine all ingredients except the peanut oil and Parmesan cheese in a blender or food processor. Process, adding the peanut oil gradually, until mixture is smooth. Add the cheese and mix until just incorporated. Serve at room temperature. To store, cover the pesto with a thin layer of peanut oil and refrigerate.

Note: The heat of Anaheim chiles varies during the course of the year. Be sure to taste one so you'll know whether to expect a mild or hot pesto.

MAKES 2 CUPS

CILANTRO PESTO

4 cups cilantro, chopped
3 cloves garlic
½ cup pine nuts, toasted (see directions
    on page xviii)
1 small jalapeño pepper, seeded and minced
    (see directions on page xix)
1 tablespoon coarse salt
¼ teaspoon freshly ground black pepper
1 tablespoon fresh lime juice
½ cup peanut oil
¼ cup freshly grated Parmesan cheese

In a blender or food processor, combine all ingredients except the peanut oil and Parmesan cheese. Process, adding the peanut oil gradually, until mixture is smooth. Add the cheese and mix until just incorporated. Serve at room temperature. To store, cover the pesto with a thin layer of peanut oil and refrigerate.

MAKES 2 CUPS

CHINESE PESTO

½ cup scallions, sliced thinly
½ cup cilantro, chopped
½ teaspoon fresh ginger, minced
1 small clove garlic, minced
1 tablespoon fresh lemon juice
1 tablespoon rice wine vinegar
1 tablespoon Teriyaki Sauce (page 7)
2 tablespoons sesame oil
¼ cup unsalted peanuts, chopped

In a blender or food processor, combine all ingredients except the peanuts. Process until smooth. Remove mixture to a small bowl and stir in peanuts just prior to serving. This pesto is best when served at room temperature the same day it is prepared.

MAKES ¾ CUP

While it's widely known that Marco Polo brought the first pasta to Italy from the Orient, some people claim he also brought pesto. It probably wasn't this recipe, but then we'll never really know. We use this pesto on our Grilled Tare-Glazed Swordfish (recipe on page 97), but it's equally good on other seafood and on grilled chicken.

SMALL PLATES

Small Plates have always been the most fun part of my menu. They're the venue where I can introduce the new and unusual because people are willing to take a chance on something small, as long as they have a sure bet picked out for their entrée.

Small Plates also reflect our new way of dining. No longer are these tempting platters limited to the role of appetizers; paired with soup or salad, you have lunch or a light dinner. Compose a meal with three or more dishes and have a gourmet "tasting" extravaganza!

DUCK AND SUN-DRIED CHERRY FAJITA

This fajita is a great way to use leftover duck but is worth the bother of making the duck from scratch! Sun-dried cherries intensify the flavors in this preparation, but you can substitute your favorite variety of fresh, pitted, or canned cherries with pleasing results.

2 tablespoons sweet butter
1 cup Maui onion, halved and sliced
½ cup red bell pepper, sliced thinly
1 cup sun-dried cherries
1 pinch crushed dried red chiles
1 cup mirin
¼ cup rice wine vinegar
¾ pound duck, boneless and skinless, cooked
    and shredded
4 (6-inch) flour tortillas, warm
½ cup sour cream

In a frypan over moderate heat, melt the butter; then, add the onion and red pepper and cook until onion begins to soften. Add the cherries and red chiles, and cook for 1 minute; add the mirin and rice wine vinegar. Continue cooking for 4–5 minutes, until cherries begin to soften, and add the cooked duck, cooking for another 2 minutes to warm the meat.

Divide mixture among the four tortillas, folding them over into a half-moon shape. Garnish with sour cream and serve.

SERVES 4

GRILLED CALAMARI STEAK WITH CILANTRO MAYO

½ cup olive oil
¼ teaspoon crushed dried red chiles
2 tablespoons fresh lime juice
2 tablespoons cilantro, chopped
2 cloves garlic, minced
6 calamari steaks (5 ounces each)
1 tablespoon coarse salt
¼ teaspoon freshly ground black pepper
6 slices toast, trimmed and quartered
1 cup Cilantro Mayo (page 16)

Calamari is one of those delicate tasting foods that is lovely when adorned with robust flavors. It's important to not overcook calamari which, when cooked too long, has a tendency to transform into rubber bands.

In a small bowl, mix the olive oil with crushed chiles, lime juice, cilantro, and garlic. Place the calamari steaks in a glass or ceramic dish, pour the olive oil mixture over them, and allow steaks to marinate at room temperature for 1 hour.

When ready to grill, remove calamari steaks from the marinade and season both sides with salt and pepper. Place on a hot grill and cook for approximately 1 minute on each side. Remove and arrange steaks on the toast points. Serve with Cilantro Mayo.

SERVES 6

GRILLED SEAFOOD SAUSAGE WITH ROASTED GARLIC BUTTER

¾ pound fillet of sole, diced
½ pound sea scallops, diced
1 tablespoon coarse salt
¼ teaspoon freshly ground black pepper
1 small egg, white only
¼ cup heavy cream
2 ounces shrimp, cleaned, deveined, and diced
    (see directions on page xix)
3 ounces lobster meat, cooked and diced
¼ cup red bell pepper, diced
¼ cup yellow bell pepper, diced
3 tablespoons cilantro, chopped
½ teaspoon lemon zest
¼ teaspoon orange zest
1 recipe Roasted Garlic Butter (page 10)

SAUSAGES

I love cooking, but I *really* love making sausages. I'm sure it has something to do with the fact that I love eating sausages, too!

My Seafood Sausage and Chicken and Cilantro Sausage demonstrate just how versatile sausage can be.

The Lamb Sausage, similar to one prepared at New York's Quilted Giraffe, has lots of cumin and garlic. Truly a sausage lover's sausage.

Place the sole, half of the scallops, the salt, pepper, and egg white in a food processor and process until smooth. Add the cream and continue processing until incorporated. Remove paste to a bowl and mix with the remaining scallops, the shrimp, lobster meat, peppers, cilantro, and citrus zests.

Place mixture in a pastry bag and pipe 5-inch sausage logs into the center of 8 individual sheets of plastic wrap. Fold the plastic wrap over and roll to encase the sausage. Twist both ends of the wrap and tie knots to form a tight package. Repeat this procedure until all the sausages are wrapped.

Bring a large saucepan of water to a boil and put in the plastic-encased sausages; lower heat to a simmer and cook for 10 minutes. Gently remove the sausages and lay them out flat to cool. Refrigerate until ready to use. (Sausages can be prepared 1 day in advance.)

When ready to serve, carefully remove the plastic wrap from each sausage. To reheat the sausages, cook over a hot grill, approximately 2–3 minutes on each side. Serve with Roasted Garlic Butter.

SERVES 4

GRILLED CHICKEN AND CILANTRO SAUSAGE WITH JALAPEÑO HONEY MUSTARD

¾ pound boneless chicken, cubed
¼ pound smoked bacon, cubed
1 bunch cilantro, chopped
3 cloves garlic
1 tablespoon fresh oregano
1 tablespoon orange zest
1 tablespoon coarse salt
1 tablespoon coarse ground black pepper
1 large egg, white only
½ cup red bell pepper, diced
1 recipe Jalapeño Honey Mustard (page 17)

Combine the chicken and bacon with the herbs and spices and chill for at least 1 hour. When chilled, run mixture through the coarse blade of a meat grinder. Gently mix with the egg white and diced red pepper until integrated. Divide into 6 equal portions and form into patties.

On a hot grill, cook the chicken sausage patties approximately 4 minutes on each side. Serve with Jalapeño Honey Mustard.

SERVES 6

GRILLED LAMB SAUSAGE
WITH CHARRED TOMATOES
AND CILANTRO PESTO

¾ pound lamb stew meat, cubed
¼ pound pork fatback, cubed
5 cloves garlic
3 tablespoons cilantro, chopped
1 tablespoon ground cumin
1 tablespoon chile powder
1 tablespoon coarse salt
1 tablespoon coarse ground black pepper
6 small tomatoes, halved
1 cup Cilantro Pesto (page 19)

Combine the lamb and fatback with the herbs and spices and chill for at least 1 hour. When chilled, run mixture through the coarse blade of a meat grinder. Gently mix until integrated; divide into 6 equal portions and form into patties.

Place the tomatoes on a hot grill, cut side up, and cook until the skins begin to char, approximately 7–10 minutes. Grill the lamb sausage patties approximately 2 minutes on each side for medium rare, or longer if you prefer them well done. Serve with the charred tomatoes and Cilantro Pesto.

SERVES 6

GRILLED SHRIMP COCKTAIL
WITH CHIPOTLE HONEY SALSA

2 cloves garlic, minced
1 small jalapeño pepper, seeded and minced,
*   (see directions on page xix)*
4 tablespoons cilantro, chopped
1 tablespoon coarse salt
¼ teaspoon freshly ground black pepper
1 tablespoon fresh lime juice
½ cup olive oil
16 jumbo shrimp, peeled and deveined
*   (see directions on page xix)*
1¼ cups Chipotle Honey Salsa (page 3)

In a food processor or blender, combine the garlic, jalapeño pepper, cilantro, salt, pepper, lime juice, and oil and process until smooth. Pour over the shrimp in a shallow dish and allow to marinate for 1 hour.

Cook the marinated shrimp over a hot grill, approximately 2 minutes on each side, until the shrimp is slightly opaque in the center. Serve warm with Chipotle Honey Salsa.

SERVES 4

Haute and spicy, this is exactly what I think a shrimp cocktail should be.

GRILLED SHRIMP TACOS WITH RADICCHIO AND AVOCADO SALSA

M y first gourmet taco.
I figured if the concept didn't
fly with grilled shrimp, it
wouldn't fly at all. After five
years these tacos are still flying
out of my kitchen.

¼ cup olive oil
2 cloves garlic, minced
12 jumbo shrimp, peeled and deveined
    (see directions on page xix)
1 tablespoon coarse salt
¼ teaspoon freshly ground black pepper
6 (8-inch) flour tortillas
12 small radicchio leaves
¾ cup Avocado Salsa (page 2)
6 wedges lime

Combine olive oil with the garlic and marinate the shrimp for
1 hour prior to grilling. When ready to cook, season shrimp with
salt and pepper and grill for approximately 1½–2 minutes on each
side, until center of shrimp is still barely opaque.

Warm the tortillas on the grill; remove to a cutting board and
cut in half. Fold one edge of tortilla half toward the center, twist-
ing that edge inside and toward the rounded top, and roll so you
have a cone-shaped tortilla. Put 1 radicchio leaf, 1 tablespoon of
Avocado Salsa, and 1 shrimp in each cone and place, seam down,
on a plate. Continue until all tacos are complete. Serve with
wedges of lime.

SERVES 6

SWEETBREADS WITH SPINACH AND WILD RICE PANCAKES AND MAUI ONION CREAM

1 pound veal sweetbreads
4 cups chicken stock
½ cup sherry
2 tablespoons coarse salt
1 recipe Spinach and Wild Rice Pancakes
    (page 133)
1 recipe Maui Onion Cream (page 12)

Place sweetbreads in a small bowl under cold running water until the water runs clear. In a small saucepan, combine the chicken stock, sherry, and salt over moderate heat, and bring up to a boil. Reduce heat to low and add the sweetbreads, poaching them for 10 minutes. Remove sweetbreads from poaching liquid and allow to cool.

When the sweetbreads are cool, remove the outer membrane and separate the lobes into equal segments. Reheat sweetbreads on a hot grill, skewering them if it makes cooking easier, for about 2 minutes on each side. Serve with Spinach and Wild Rice Pancakes and Maui Onion Cream.

SERVES 4

There are sweetbread lovers and sweetbread haters and a lot of people who don't realize this has nothing to do with "sweet breads" at all.

Sweetbreads is a name for the thymus gland, a delicately flavored organ meat that lends itself to being paired with a wide variety of sauces. It's extremely rich. My general feeling is that if you're going to blow your diet, you might as well go all the way, so I managed to pair this with my grandmother's Spinach and Wild Rice Pancakes, which are cooked in butter, and the heavenly rich Maui Onion Cream.

KIM CHEE CRAB MARTINI

For years I avoided putting seafood cocktails on my menus because I wanted everything to be new. Seafood cocktails are too often relics left on menus for familiarity and comfort's sake, their preparation taken as much for granted as the red sauce with which they are so often served.

A little fun with words, a little work with food, and my Kim Chee Crab Martini was launched. Kim chee is spicy marinated cabbage, a Korean specialty. I adopted its marinade to make the mayonnaise I use in my martini. (This mayonnaise is also excellent when used as a cocktail sauce for chilled seafood.) You may adjust the amount of heat by increasing or decreasing the amount of kim chee marinade.

A bit of gin inevitably became part of the recipe, and the garnish of a crab claw clutching a green olive simply couldn't be resisted.

1½ pounds fresh lump crabmeat, cooked
6 cups Napa cabbage, sliced thinly
¼ cup mint leaves
1 recipe Kim Chee Mayo
6 large cocktail crab claws
6 large pimento-stuffed green olives

In a small bowl, combine the crabmeat with the cabbage and mint leaves. Toss with the Kim Chee Mayo until evenly mixed. Divide the mixture among 6 oversized martini glasses, and garnish each with a crab claw "clutching" an olive.

SERVES 6

KIM CHEE MAYO

2 tablespoons sugar
¼ cup water
1 teaspoon fresh lemon juice
⅔ cup mayonnaise
1 tablespoon rice wine vinegar
2 tablespoons gin
½ cup kim chee marinade

In a small saucepan over moderate heat, combine the sugar, water, and lemon juice. Bring to a boil and remove from the heat immediately. Cool before using in the next step.

Combine the cooled syrup with the remaining ingredients in a small bowl and mix until integrated. Refrigerated, keeps up to a month.

MAKES 1½ CUPS

LOBSTER ROLLS WITH BACON AND SWEET CORN

6 slices smoked bacon
2 cloves garlic, minced
1 cup onion, sliced thinly
1 cup fresh corn kernels
¼ cup red bell pepper, diced
2 cups Napa cabbage, sliced thinly
1 tablespoon fresh tarragon leaves, whole
1 tablespoon coarse salt
¼ teaspoon freshly ground black pepper
6 ounces lobster meat, cooked, diced
8 eggroll skins
1 egg white
oil for frying
1 recipe Chinese Hot Mustard (page 9)

In a frypan over moderate heat, cook the bacon until crisp. Remove bacon from the pan and cook garlic and onion in the bacon fat until translucent. Remove the onion and garlic mixture and place in a mixing bowl until it cools to room temperature. Chop the bacon coarsely and add to the cooled onion mixture along with the corn, red pepper, cabbage, tarragon, and lobster meat. Season with salt and pepper and mix until integrated.

Lay out the eggroll wrappers and brush the edges with egg white. Divide the filling equally, placing mixture along the center of each wrapper diagonally, leaving a 2-inch border on all sides. Carefully, fold two points over the ends of the log; then, place one point over the length of the log and roll, making sure the wrapper encases the filling tightly. Repeat until all the egg rolls are made.

Place two inches of oil in a saucepan and heat until oil reaches 350 degrees. Fry the egg rolls until golden brown on each side. Drain on a paper towel to remove excess oil. Serve with Chinese Hot Mustard.

SERVES 4

BAJA FISH TACOS

Very soon after moving to San Diego I took a day trip to Ensenada, Mexico, in Baja California, and treated myself to their roadside specialty known simply as "fish tacos." They changed my whole perception of tacos. What tacos can be is limited only by your imagination. Making a taco is no different than building a sandwich: pick your bread, be it flour or corn tortillas, decide upon a filling, and then choose a suitable salsa.

This recipe is a reasonable facsimile of the fish tacos that I first tasted in Ensenada. What I couldn't duplicate was the atmosphere provided by those curbside taco stands, complete with sunny sky, ocean breezes, and the sounds and colors of the marketplace.

For a variation, try grilling the fish on your barbecue. Although the recipe specifies sea bass, any firm, white-fleshed fish will do as well as shark or swordfish. Don't fail to give them a squeeze of fresh lime!

BEER BATTER

½ cup flour
1½ tablespoons paprika
¼ teaspoon freshly ground black pepper
2 tablespoons cornstarch
2 teaspoons coarse salt
½ teaspoon granulated garlic
1 cup beer, cold

oil for frying
¾ pound sea bass fillet
½ cup flour
1 cup green cabbage, shredded
8 (6-inch) corn tortillas, warmed
½ cup Cilantro Mayo (page 16)
½ cup Fresh Tomato Salsa (page 2)
8 wedges lime

To make the batter, sift all dry ingredients into a small bowl and whisk in the beer gradually until batter is smooth. Keep refrigerated until ready to use.

In a heavy frypan, heat 2 inches of oil to 350 degrees. Cut the sea bass into 8 strips, dredge in flour, cover completely with beer batter, and place carefully in the hot oil, frying on both sides until golden brown. Remove and drain excess oil on paper towels.

To assemble the tacos, place equal amounts of cabbage down the center of each warm tortilla; then, put a tablespoon of Cilantro Mayo, a strip of fried sea bass, and, finally, a tablespoon of Fresh Tomato Salsa. Serve with lime wedges.

SERVES 4

BUFFALO MOZZARELLA WITH MEXICAN BEER SALSA

2 large eggs
2 tablespoons water
12 ounces buffalo mozzarella, cut into 4
    3-ounce slices
½ cup flour
2 cups panko bread crumbs
3 tablespoons sweet butter
2 cups Mexican Beer Salsa (page 4)

If you can accept the concept of Spaghetti Westerns, you may enjoy my southwestern adaptation of Italian fried mozzarella with marinara sauce.

On a shallow plate, stir the eggs with the water well. Dredge mozzarella through the flour, cover completely with the egg wash, and coat with the panko bread crumbs.

Heat butter in a medium-sized frypan over moderate heat and pan-fry the cheese until golden brown, approximately 3–4 minutes on each side. Serve with warmed Mexican Beer Salsa.

SERVES 4

MANGO, JALAPEÑO, AND BRIE QUESADILLA

This recipe's combination of sweet and hot, along with the creaminess of brie, is a great flavor treat! Make sure the mango you use is ripe; if not ripe or mangoes are not available, try using sweet pineapple.

4 (8-inch) flour tortillas
12 ounces brie cheese, room temperature
1 medium ripe mango, peeled and diced
8 pickled jalapeño peppers, seeded and diced
(see directions on page xix)
½ cup cilantro, chopped
¼ cup sour cream

Preheat oven to 350 degrees. Lay the tortillas out flat on a cookie sheet. Remove the skin from the brie and distribute the cheese equally among the tortillas, spreading out from the center until it covers all but a 1-inch border around the tortilla's diameter. Randomly distribute the mango, jalapeño peppers, and cilantro over the tortillas.

Place cookie sheet in the oven and bake for 5–7 minutes, just until the cheese has melted.

Cut each quesadilla into 4 pizza-style slices, place on individual plates, garnish with sour cream, and serve.

SERVES 4

MAUI ONION FRITTERS
WITH PINEAPPLE SALSA

1 cup flour
2 teaspoons paprika
1 teaspoon baking powder
1 teaspoon coarse salt
½ teaspoon freshly ground black pepper
2 eggs
1 cup beer, cold
2 cups Maui onion, halved and sliced
2 tablespoons fresh tarragon leaves
½ cup red bell pepper, diced small
oil for frying
1 recipe Pineapple Salsa (page 6)

Sift the flour, paprika, baking powder, salt, and pepper in a small mixing bowl. Make a well in the center, add the eggs and beer, and mix gently until combined. Into this mixture, fold the onion, tarragon, and red bell pepper.

In a deep frypan, add 2 inches of oil and heat to 350 degrees. Carefully, add fritter batter to the oil, using a fork, and flatten to form 3-inch round fritters. Cook until golden brown on both sides. Serve with Pineapple Salsa.

SERVES 6

These fritters resemble onion rings more than fritters, which are sometimes too doughy. You can use any variety of onion, but the sweet Maui onion, and some of the other sweet varieties, really make this dish special. Because they are so good, we created our Pineapple Salsa, which lets the flavor of the onion shine through.

STEAMED MUSSELS WITH TOMATO HERB SALSA

New Zealand green lip is our choice of mussel to use, but this recipe will be a success with any variety of mussel that is available to you. Be sure to use fresh herbs in the Tomato Herb Salsa, which is so versatile that it can be used cold as a topping for chilled seafood or hot as a salsa for steamed shellfish and chicken. It's essential that you serve this dish with a good bread to mop up the sauce.

2 tablespoons olive oil
4 pounds mussels, cleaned (see directions
    on page xix)
½ cup dry vermouth
1 recipe Tomato Herb Salsa
8 tablespoons (1 stick) sweet butter, cold
4 wedges lemon

Place a large saucepan over high heat and add olive oil; when oil just begins to smoke, add the mussels and cover. Continuing over high heat, cook the mussels for 2 minutes; then, lower to moderate heat, add the vermouth, Tomato Herb Salsa, butter, and cover again. Cook an additional 4–6 minutes, until all the mussels have opened.

Divide the mussels equally into soup bowls and pour any broth remaining in the pan over them. Serve with lemon wedges.

SERVES 4

TOMATO HERB SALSA

4 cups tomatoes, seeded and diced
2 tablespoons fresh parsley, chopped
2 tablespoons fresh tarragon, chopped
2 tablespoons fresh basil, chopped
2 tablespoons fresh chive, chopped
2 tablespoons white wine vinegar
4 cloves garlic, minced
½ teaspoon freshly ground black pepper
1 tablespoon coarse salt
¼ cup olive oil

In a large bowl, mix all ingredients together. Before using, allow salsa to sit 2 hours at room temperature for flavors to meld.

MAKES 4½ CUPS

BAKED OYSTERS WITH CILANTRO PESTO

20 large fresh oysters
1 recipe Cilantro Pesto (page 19)
4 large lemon wedges

Preheat oven on broil setting. Clean and shuck oysters and place them on the half shell. Put a generous tablespoon of Cilantro Pesto over each oyster. Place on a broiler pan and cook under broiler for 3–5 minutes, until pesto just begins to bubble and brown lightly. Remove from oven and serve with lemon wedges.

SERVES 4

I'm not a real fan of oysters, but this simple rendition of baked oysters entices even me.

POTATO-ONION QUESADILLA

QUESADILLAS

Translated literally, quesadillas are "cheese cakes." Why they haven't reached popularity of the epic proportions that pizza has, I'll never know. They're easier to prepare and equally adaptable to a rainbow of ingredients.

Try your own variations with different cheeses and toppings, and if you're partial to corn tortillas, go right ahead and use them!

This adaptation of a Mexican regional specialty is one of my favorites. Great for a snack or appetizer and unique as a side dish with an entrée. It's Mexican comfort food at its best.

¾ pound baking potatoes
2 tablespoons coarse salt
2 cups onion, sliced
2 cloves garlic, minced
6 tablespoons sweet butter
3 ounces havarti cheese, grated
¼ teaspoon freshly ground black pepper
4 (8-inch) flour tortillas
½ cup sour cream

Wash the potatoes; cut them, leaving skins on, into smaller pieces; place in a saucepan with 1 tablespoon of the salt; and cover with water. Over high heat, boil potatoes until they are cooked through, approximately 7–10 minutes; remove from heat and drain thoroughly.

While potatoes are cooking, sauté the onion and garlic in 2 tablespoons of the butter until onions are browned lightly. While hot, combine the drained potatoes and sautéed onions in a mixing bowl with the cheese, 2 tablespoons butter, the remaining salt, and pepper and mix as if making mashed potatoes.

Divide potato mixture into 4 equal portions. Spread the mixture over half of each tortilla, folding the other half over to create a half-moon shape.

Melt the remaining butter in a frypan over moderate heat and sauté the quesadillas 2–3 minutes on each side, until golden brown. Garnish with sour cream and serve.

SERVES 4

Takoshimi of Peppered Ahi with Chinese Salsa (recipe on page 42) ⇒

SHRIMP MACHACA

3 tablespoons peanut oil
1 cup onion, diced
½ cup Anaheim chile, seeded and diced
 (see directions on page xix)
1 small Jalapeño pepper, seeded and minced
 (see directions on page xix)
1 teaspoon dried oregano
1 pound shrimp meat, chopped coarsely
2 cups tomatoes, seeded and diced
½ cup chicken stock
2 teaspoons coarse salt
¼ teaspoon freshly ground black pepper
12 (6-inch) flour tortillas, warmed

Heat peanut oil in a large frypan over moderate heat and sauté onion, chile, and pepper until softened. Add oregano and cook for 1 minute; then, add the shrimp meat. While stirring, cook an additional minute before adding the tomatoes and chicken stock. Continue cooking until almost all liquid has evaporated from the pan. Season with salt and pepper and serve with the warmed flour tortillas.

SERVES 6

⇐ *Mango, Jalapeño, and Brie Quesadilla (recipe on page 34)*

Machaca usually refers to Mexican dried beef. I came across a recipe in a regional Mexican cookbook that used shrimp in a machacalike preparation and adapted it to this home-style dish, which is a remote cousin to shrimp provençale.

SMOKED CHICKEN AND ROASTED RED PEPPER QUESADILLA

Go ahead and substitute left-over chicken for the smoked variety, or even eliminate the chicken altogether, but be sure you take the time to roast your own peppers.

4 (8-inch) flour tortillas
12 ounces Monterey Jack cheese
½ pound smoked chicken, shredded
2 large red bell peppers, roasted, peeled,
    and cut into long slices (see directions on
    page xix)
½ cup scallions, sliced thinly
1½ cups Avocado Salsa (page 2)

Lay the tortillas flat on a cookie sheet. Slice and distribute the cheese equally among the tortillas, until it covers all but a 1-inch border around the diameter. Distribute the smoked chicken, roasted pepper, and the scallions over the tortillas. Place cookie sheet in the oven and bake just until the cheese has melted, approximately 5–7 minutes.

Cut each quesadilla into 4 pizza-style slices and place on individual plates. Serve with Avocado Salsa on the side.

SERVES 4

SMOKED SHRIMP AND CREAMY HAVARTI QUESADILLA

4 (8-inch) flour tortillas
12 ounces havarti cheese
16 large smoked shrimp
½ cup sun-dried tomatoes, sliced
½ cup cilantro, chopped
1½ cups Avocado Salsa (page 2)

Preheat oven to 350 degrees. Lay the tortillas out flat on a cookie sheet. Slice the cheese and distribute equally among the tortillas, until it covers all but a 1-inch border around the diameter. Distribute the smoked shrimp, sun-dried tomatoes, and cilantro over the tortillas.

Place cookie sheet in the oven and bake just until the cheese has melted, approximately 5–7 minutes. Cut each quesadilla into 4 pizza-style slices, and place on individual plates. Serve with Avocado Salsa on the side.

SERVES 4

We marinate shrimp in our Smoky Barbeque Salsa and then smoke slowly with hickory wood. If that's too much planning and you need a quick fix, you can always substitute cooked shrimp, crab, or lobster with pleasing results.

TAKOSHIMI OF PEPPERED AHI WITH CHINESE SALSA

Living in southern California, it was inevitable that I create a taco with *sashimi*, raw fish. Since sashimi is Oriental, I felt the taco should be made with Oriental ingredients.

Coming up with the ingredients was easy: I substituted wonton skins for tortillas, used the highest quality ahi (yellowfin) tuna, and flavored the traditional tomato salsa with shiitake mushrooms, soy sauce, and sesame oil. (Make it a point to tell your fish market you want sashimi-grade ahi. If it's not available, don't hesitate to substitute beef tenderloin, preparing it in exactly the same fashion. If you can't get shiitake mushrooms, use any type of fresh mushroom available.)

But naming the taco "Takoshimi" really gave this dish its unique identity. Maureen Clancy, *San Diego Union* food editor, voted it as 1990's Dish of the Year, making it one of the decade's ten best.

1 cup plus 1 tablespoon peanut oil
18 fresh wonton skins
1 pound sashimi-grade ahi
6 tablespoons coarse ground black pepper
4 tablespoons coarse salt
3 cups Napa cabbage, sliced
¾ cup Chinese Salsa

In a small saucepan, heat 1 cup of the peanut oil to 350 degrees. One at a time, place the wonton skins in the oil, and with a pair of tongs, fold skin in half while it is frying so it takes the form of a taco shell. The shell should turn a light golden brown color before it is removed and placed on a paper towel to drain. Repeat the procedure until all shells are prepared. Set aside until needed.

Coat the tuna generously with the coarse pepper and salt. Place a frypan over high heat and add the 1 tablespoon oil. When the oil starts to smoke, place the tuna carefully in the pan and sear for 30 seconds on each side. Remove from the pan. When cool enough to handle, slice tuna into 18 equal portions.

To assemble the taco, divide the Napa cabbage equally among the wonton shells, placing on the bottom; follow with a slice of tuna; and top with a generous tablespoon of Chinese Salsa.

Serve immediately as the taco shell will get soggy from the moisture of the salsa.

SERVES 6

CHINESE SALSA

1 tablespoon sweet butter
2 cloves garlic, minced
2 cups fresh shiitake mushrooms, sliced
½ cup Teriyaki Sauce (page 7)
1 cup tomatoes, diced
½ cup scallions, sliced thinly
½ teaspoon chile and garlic paste
¼ cup rice wine vinegar
2 tablespoons sesame oil
¼ teaspoon freshly ground black pepper
1 bunch cilantro, chopped

Melt butter in a sauté pan; add garlic and cook gently for 1 minute. Add the sliced shiitake mushrooms and continue cooking over low heat until mushrooms become tender. Add the Teriyaki Sauce, bring to a boil quickly, and remove from heat. Allow mushrooms to cool to room temperature.

In a separate bowl, combine all remaining ingredients and mix well. When mushrooms have cooled, combine with the tomato mixture. Serve at room temperature. Refrigerated, mixture will keep for several days.

MAKES 3 CUPS

SOUTHWESTERN POTSTICKERS

There's an entire market basket of ingredients common to the American Southwest, Latin America, and Asia. Though the individual cooking styles from these geographic areas are quite unique, the shared ground invites the fusing of the cuisines. These Chinese pan-fried dumplings with accents of southwestern flavor are a prime example.

1 medium Anaheim chile, seeded and chopped
    (see directions on page xix)
2 cloves garlic
¼ cup cilantro, chopped
2 tablespoons freshly grated Parmesan cheese
2 tablespoons pine nuts
¾ pound chicken breast, boneless and skinless
2 egg whites
1 tablespoon coarse salt
½ teaspoon garlic and chile paste
½ cup plus 2 tablespoons Teriyaki Sauce
    (page 7)
2 tablespoons yellow bell pepper, diced
2 tablespoons red bell pepper, diced
2 tablespoons celery, diced
2 tablespoons jicama, diced
30 round dumpling skins
2 tablespoons sweet butter
½ cup water
1 recipe Sweet Corn Cream (page 13)

Combine the Anaheim chile, garlic, cilantro, Parmesan cheese, and pine nuts in a food processor and pulse until uniformly chopped. Add the chicken, 1 of the egg whites, salt, garlic and chile paste, and 2 tablespoons of the Teriyaki Sauce and process until the mixture is smooth. Remove to a small bowl and mix in the diced peppers, celery, and jicama.

Lay out the dumpling skins on a large surface. One at a time, brush each skin with some of the remaining egg white. Place approximately 1 tablespoon of the chicken mixture in the center of each dumpling skin, fold over like a turnover, and pat edges to seal. Continue until all dumplings are made.

In a large frypan over moderate heat, melt butter and place dumplings with seam side up. Cook 1½ minutes, until the skins begin to brown on the bottom side. Add the remaining Teriyaki Sauce and water to the pan, cover, and allow to steam 4 minutes. Remove from pan and serve with Sweet Corn Cream.

SERVES 6

WILD MUSHROOM FAJITA

2 cloves garlic, minced
½ cup onion, sliced thinly
2 tablespoons sweet butter
1 tablespoon fresh thyme, chopped
1 teaspoon fresh basil, chopped
1 teaspoon fresh oregano, chopped
¼ cup red bell pepper, sliced thinly
6 cups assorted wild mushrooms, sliced
½ tablespoon coarse salt
½ teaspoon freshly ground black pepper
4 (6-inch) flour tortillas, warmed
4 tablespoons sour cream

In a large frypan over moderate heat, cook the garlic and onion in the butter until translucent. Add the herbs and cook another minute; then, add the red pepper, mushrooms, salt, and pepper. Cook approximately 3–5 minutes until mushrooms are tender. Portion out equal amounts of the mushroom filling into the warm tortillas, folding over in a half-moon shape to cover the filling. Garnish each fajita with a tablespoon of the sour cream.

SERVES 4

FAJITAS

Normally, if the popularity of a dish reaches such proportions that one of the national food chains picks up on it, it would signal the end to my serving that dish at Pacifica Grill, no matter how distinct my variation.

In this case, I added fajitas to my menu *after* such an occurrence. Fajitas are a California creation that usually consist of steak or chicken and onions and peppers, served with warm tortillas on a sizzling platter.

My fajitas update a few classics such as mushrooms on toast and duckling Montmorency.

CARIBBEAN CRAB CAKES
WITH SWEET LIME SALSA

I tasted nothing like these in the Caribbean, but the flavors of the islands provided a new rhythm and alternative to the classic Maryland-style crab cake. Like a lot of my cooking, this recipe blends something old with something new.

The salsa, which packs a little kick because of the addition of jerk spice, has an overall soothing effect, the result of the sweetened lime juice. Besides being the perfect complement for these crab cakes, this salsa is an interesting accompaniment to chicken and an unusual baste for barbecue ribs.

½ pound fresh lump crabmeat
¼ cup onion, minced
¼ cup red bell pepper, minced
2 tablespoons Caribbean jerk spice
2 teaspoons honey
½ cup mayonnaise
1 cup fresh bread crumbs
3 tablespoons sweet butter
1 recipe Sweet Lime Salsa

In a small bowl, gently mix all ingredients except the butter and salsa, until combined. Form into 12 crab cakes.

In a frypan over moderate heat, cook the crab cakes in the butter until golden brown on both sides. Serve with Sweet Lime Salsa.

SERVES 6

SWEET LIME SALSA

¼ cup sugar
1 tablespoon water
1 cup Rose's Lime Juice
2 small limes, unpeeled and sliced thinly
2 teaspoons Caribbean jerk spice
2 teaspoons rice wine vinegar

In a small saucepan over moderate heat, combine the sugar and water and cook until sugar caramelizes to a light golden brown. Carefully add the lime juice, limes, jerk spice, and rice wine vinegar and continue cooking over low heat for 15 minutes. Serve at room temperature.

MAKES 1 CUP

CASSEROLE OF ESCARGOT WITH GARLIC AND FENNEL

½ cup mushrooms, diced
2 tablespoons sweet butter
½ cup fresh fennel, diced
½ cup leeks, diced
4 cloves garlic, minced
½ cup tomatoes, seeded and diced
¼ cup white wine
2 cups heavy cream
2 tablespoons coarse salt
¼ teaspoon freshly ground black pepper
24 large escargots, washed to remove brine

In a small frypan over moderate heat, sauté the mushrooms in butter until the moisture from the mushrooms is released. Add the fennel, leeks, and garlic and continue cooking until leeks are tender. Add the tomatoes and wine; cook until almost all the moisture has evaporated. Add the cream, bring to a boil, and simmer 10 minutes. Season mixture with salt and pepper, add the escargots, and cook gently for 1 minute, just long enough to warm the escargots.

Remove from heat, divide escargots and sauce into individual ramekins, and serve.

SERVES 4

There are those people who contend that escargot is prepared as an excuse to dunk bread in garlic butter. This recipe provides an alternative for those who would prefer dunking in a garlic and fennel cream.

CASSOULET OF LOBSTER WITH SPICY ORIENTAL BLACK BEAN SALSA

¾ pound lobster meat, cooked
1 recipe Spicy Oriental Black Bean Salsa
*   (page 8)*
4 (6-inch) puff pastry rounds
1 large egg
1 tablespoon water

Preheat oven to 375 degrees. Divide the lobster meat and *cold* Spicy Oriental Black Bean Salsa equally among 4 baking ramekins.

Beat the egg and water together, and brush the wash lightly around the outside edge of each ramekin. Place a round of puff pastry over each ramekin, pressing the edges of the pastry down firmly so a tight seal is formed. Brush puff pastry with the remaining egg wash.

For best results, cover and chill the ramekins for at least 15 minutes prior to baking. Place ramekins in the oven, bake until the pastry is golden brown, approximately 15–18 minutes, and serve.

SERVES 4

This dish has very little in common with the traditional French cassoulet, but I like the sound of its name. What the heck! It tastes good, and adding a French pastry lid to this otherwise Asian-inspired dish, makes a most interesting potpie.

CRUSTED SOFT-SHELL CRAB WITH AVOCADO AND CHIPOTLE HONEY

2 large avocados, peeled and pitted
1 tablespoon fresh lime juice
½ cup honey
¼ cup tomato paste
1 teaspoon canned chipotle chile, puréed
1 large egg
2 tablespoons water
4 large fresh soft-shell crabs, cleaned
*   (see directions on page xix)*
¼ cup flour
1 cup red tortilla chips, crushed
4 tablespoons (½ stick) sweet butter

In a food processor or blender, process the avocado and lime juice until completely smooth. Set aside. Mix the honey, tomato paste, and chipotle chile purée in a small bowl until combined.

In separate bowl, combine the egg and water, mixing well with a fork. Dredge the crab, shell side only, by passing through the egg wash, the flour, and finally the tortilla crumbs, making sure to press crab into the crumbs so they adhere.

In a skillet over moderate heat, melt the butter and add the crab. Cook approximately 3 minutes on each side, shell side first, until done.

To serve, distribute the avocado purée among 4 plates, place soft-shell crab on top of the avocado bed, and drizzle chipotle honey over the crab.

SERVES 4

When the waters of the Atlantic begin to warm, these blue crabs shed their hard shells in favor of a new summer wardrobe that, for a few days, is so lightweight we can eat the *whole* thing. If you can't get soft-shell crabs where you live, they're worth planning a trip to Maryland.

The refreshing quality of avocado and the spice of the chipotle chile enhance the delicate flavor of the crab, as does the red tortilla crust. You can substitute yellow corn tortillas if red are not available.

CRAB ENCHILADAS
WITH ROASTED GARLIC CREAM

The sweetness of Dungeness crab combined with the nutty quality of Roasted Garlic Cream elevates the enchilada to new heights. Prepare enchiladas a day in advance and bake off when needed. This recipe is also great when you use cooked chicken, shrimp, or steak, in place of the crabmeat.

2 pounds Dungeness crabmeat, cooked
2 cups celery, diced and blanched
2 cups leeks, diced and blanched
2 recipes Roasted Garlic Cream (page 11)
12 (6-inch) flour tortillas
2 tablespoons sweet butter
¾ cup Monterey Jack cheese, shredded

Preheat oven to 350 degrees. In a small bowl, combine the crabmeat, celery, leeks, and half of the Roasted Garlic Cream and mix until well combined. Divide the mixture equally among the 12 tortillas and roll them into logs.

Place the enchiladas, seam side down, side by side in a buttered shallow baking dish. Pour the remaining sauce over the enchiladas, sprinkle the shredded cheese, and bake, uncovered, for 25–30 minutes until top begins to brown. Serve, pouring any Roasted Garlic Cream remaining in the baking dish over the enchiladas.

SERVES 6

ORANGE-AND-GINGER-GLAZED LAMB RIBLETS

4 racks lamb ribs (about 2 pounds total)
2 cups hoisin sauce
6 cups orange juice
¼ cup fresh ginger, minced

Preheat oven to 375 degrees. Cut lamb racks into individual ribs. Combine the hoisin sauce with the orange juice and ginger. Reserve 1½ cups of the sauce mixture, pouring the rest over the lamb ribs in a roasting pan. Place pan in the oven and cook for approximately 1½ hours, stirring every 15 minutes, until ribs begin to get crusty and well glazed. Remove ribs from the roasting pan, drain any fat, heat the reserved sauce, and serve.

SERVES 4

BARBEQUED RIBS

Ribs are in one of those categories of food that has fanatic followers. I'm, therefore, not even going to bother trying to convince anyone how great these ribs are; however, they are my favorite.

I use lamb ribs, not only because they offer a more distinctive flavor, but they are often more reasonably priced. Ask your butcher to trim away any excess fat to save yourself the trouble. If you prefer, you can use pork or beef ribs—just make sure to adjust the cooking time to ensure that the meat is nice and tender.

This recipe is from the now-defunct New York City restaurant, Lavin's. It was one of their most requested featured appetizers. You will enjoy this variation of the traditional ribs served in most Chinese restaurants.

CHILE-CRUSTED LAMB RIBLETS WITH BURNT ORANGE SAUCE

When I created this recipe, I wanted to emphasize the crusty quality of ribs without ending up with a tough or burned product. By creating the crust with spices, I managed to achieve what I wanted and came up with a truly unique style of ribs, too.

If you're good at burning things, don't think you've finally found the perfect sauce. The Burnt Orange Sauce begins with a caramel base, which if truly burnt, will taste just as bad as burnt toast. This sauce is used to cool the chiles on the ribs and is well suited as a sweet dipping sauce to contrast other spicy, or not so spicy, dishes that you prepare.

4 racks lamb ribs (about 2 pounds total)
1 medium onion, peeled and quartered
1 large carrot, cut roughly
1 stalk celery, cut roughly
10 whole black peppercorns
1 bay leaf
½ cup chile powder
2 tablespoons ground cumin
2 tablespoons granulated garlic
2 tablespoons coarse salt
1 tablespoon dried mustard
1 tablespoon freshly ground black pepper
1 tablespoon dried thyme leaves
½ cup dark brown sugar
8 tablespoons (1 stick) sweet butter, melted
1 recipe Burnt Orange Sauce

Place rib racks with the onion, carrot, celery, peppercorns, and bay leaf in a large saucepan; cover with water, bring to a boil, and simmer gently until ribs are tender, 1½–2 hours. Remove racks from the water and allow to cool.

Preheat oven to 375 degrees. Combine the remaining spices, herbs, and brown sugar in a small bowl, add the melted butter and mix until well integrated.

On the top side of each rib rack, distribute the chile mixture evenly and pat firmly to create an even crust. Place the rib racks on a cookie sheet, put in oven, and cook for 20 minutes. Serve with Burnt Orange Sauce.

SERVES 4

BURNT ORANGE SAUCE

¼ cup sugar
1 cup fresh orange juice
1 teaspoon orange zest
1 teaspoon fresh lemon juice
½ teaspoon Angostura aromatic bitters
1 clove garlic, minced
¼ teaspoon fresh ginger, minced
¼ teaspoon dry mustard
¼ teaspoon freshly ground black pepper

In a saucepan over moderate heat, combine the sugar with 1 tablespoon of the orange juice and caramelize the sugar until it turns a rich golden brown. Remove from the heat and *carefully* (because the hot caramel will splatter!) add the remaining orange juice; then, add the rest of the ingredients. Return to the stove top, bring mixture to a boil, and allow it to simmer gently for 10 minutes. Chill before serving.

MAKES 1¼ CUPS

THE S COURSE

Whenever I write menus, I place soups and salads in a category of their own rather than including them with the appetizers. Soups and salads are the stuff meals are made of. They provide a perfect balance of food that, on one hand, is rich and satisfying, and on the other, light and zesty.

I've met a lot of people who consider soup to be restaurant food, not something they would prepare from scratch at home, which they assume to be either too difficult or time-consuming. Perhaps they associate soup making with the long, arduous task of making stocks before one even begins preparing the soup. The following recipes demonstrate that you can eliminate this step and create stellar soups in less than an hour.

Salads often get the rap of being rabbit food. Rabbits should eat so well! My salads are created to surprise and excite those people who tend to order salads as a safe alternative to some of my more adventurous dishes.

PINEAPPLE GAZPACHO

In cooking, availability is the true mother of invention. In this gazpacho recipe, pineapple makes a surprising and refreshing substitution for the traditional tomato.

1 medium yellow bell pepper
2 medium red bell peppers
1 medium red onion
2 large cucumbers, seeded
1 large pineapple, peeled and cored
1 cup daikon
2 cloves garlic, minced
½ cup cilantro, chopped
¼ cup fresh lime juice
½ cup fresh orange juice
1 cup mirin
2 cups pineapple juice
½ cup olive oil
½ teaspoon chile and garlic paste
¼ teaspoon freshly ground black pepper

Divide the peppers, onion, cucumbers, pineapple, and daikon into two equal groups. Dice one group finely and liquify the other in a food processor or blender.

Combine the diced and liquified vegetables in a large noncorrosive bowl and stir in the remaining ingredients. Chill before serving.

SERVES 6

GAZPACHO GOLD

3 pints yellow cherry tomatoes
1 clove garlic
1 small jalapeño pepper, seeded and minced
    (see directions on page xix)
1 bunch cilantro, chopped
1 cup yellow bell pepper, diced
1 cup red bell pepper, diced
1 cup cucumber, peeled, seeded, and diced
½ cup jicama, diced
½ cup red onion, diced
¾ cup rice wine vinegar
¼ cup white wine
⅛ cup olive oil
2 teaspoons coarse salt
¼ teaspoon freshly ground black pepper
6 tablespoons sour cream
2 tablespoons fresh chives, chopped

The yellow tomato again makes an appearance in one of my recipes. I'm not addicted to them, I just like being a little different, especially when the difference brings a marked improvement in flavor to an old standard.

In a food processor or blender, combine all of the yellow tomatoes, garlic, jalapeño, cilantro and half of the diced peppers, cucumbers, jicama, and red onion; process until the mixture is liquified.

Remove to a mixing bowl, add the remaining half of the diced vegetables, the vinegar, wine, and oil; and stir until combined. Season with salt and pepper. Chill. When ready to serve, ladle into bowls and garnish each with a tablespoon of sour cream and the chives.

SERVES 6

SOUTHWESTERN
BLACK BEAN SOUP

This soup has become a fixture on our menu, though it has changed its appearance over the years. If you like more texture, you can purée only part of the beans, or none of them. For variations in flavor, try simmering this soup, or the Basic Black Beans, with smoked turkey or ham.

1 recipe Basic Black Beans (page 128)
2 cups chicken stock or water
6 tablespoons sour cream
6 tablespoons scallions, sliced thinly

In a food processor or blender, purée the Basic Black Beans until smooth. Combine the puréed beans and chicken stock in a saucepan, and over low heat, bring mixture to a boil, stirring occasionally. Remove from heat and serve, garnishing each with a tablespoon of sour cream and the scallions.

SERVES 6

NO-BEAN CHILE

¼ pound smoked bacon, diced
1 pound beef steak, cut into ½-inch cubes
2 cups onion, diced
3 cups Anaheim chile, seeded and diced
    (see directions on page xix)
3 cloves garlic, minced
1 teaspoon fresh thyme, chopped
1 teaspoon fresh oregano, chopped
1 bunch cilantro, chopped
2 tablespoons ground cumin
1 cup green olives stuffed with jalapeño pepper,
    chopped
1 cup fresh tomatoes, seeded and diced
2 bottles beer (12 ounces each)
2 cups water
2 tablespoons coarse salt
½ teaspoon freshly ground black pepper
1 teaspoon habañero chile sauce
¾ cup cheddar cheese, grated

There's nothing wrong with beans in chile. And there's nothing wrong with chile without beans! This Santa Fe style green chile is moderate in heat but full in flavor. If you don't have bottled habañero chile sauce available to you, you can substitute your favorite brand, but you'll miss out on the unique flavor of this variety of chile, which is the hottest chile in the Americas.

In a large saucepan over medium heat, cook the bacon until it is crisp and the fat is rendered. Add the cubed beef steak and cook until browned evenly, add the onion and Anaheim chile and cook, stirring occasionally, for another 4 minutes. Stir in the garlic, herbs, and cumin, cooking for another minute; then, add the olives, tomatoes, beer, and water. Bring mixture to a boil and simmer for 45 minutes over low heat. Season with salt, pepper, and habañero chile sauce and serve. Garnish each serving with grated cheese.

SERVES 6

JAPANESE CLAM AND
WATER CHESTNUT CHOWDER

Clam chowders, be they the cream or tomato variety, are restaurant standards. Presented with the dilemma of satisfying our patrons' wishes for chowder on the menu and my wishes to fulfill the concept of Pacific Rim cookery, I came up with this chowder, which has neither cream, tomatoes, nor the usual prerequisite potato.

To my way of thinking, if they served clam chowder in Japan, this would be it!

6 tablespoons (3/4 stick) sweet butter
1/4 cup leeks, diced
2 cloves garlic, minced
1 1/2 cups shiitake mushrooms
1/2 cup flour
1/4 cup Teriyaki Sauce (page 7)
3 cups clam juice
1 can (10 1/2 ounces) chopped clams with juice
1 can (8 ounces) water chestnuts, sliced
1/2 cup scallions, sliced thinly
2 tablespoons fresh lemon juice
1/4 tablespoon freshly ground black pepper

Melt the butter in a saucepan over moderate heat, add the leeks and garlic, and cook, stirring occasionally, for 3 minutes. Add the mushrooms and continue cooking for 3 more minutes. Stir in the flour until it absorbs all the liquid in the pot; then, add the Teriyaki Sauce, clam juice, chopped clams, water chestnuts, and scallions. Bring the mixture to a boil. Lower the heat and simmer soup for 20 minutes. Add the lemon juice and black pepper and serve.

SERVES 4

CREAM OF CILANTRO SOUP

2 tablespoons sweet butter
3 cloves garlic, minced
1 cup onion, diced
1 cup celery, diced
4 tablespoons flour
3 cups milk
1 cup heavy cream
2 cups cilantro, chopped
1 tablespoon coarse salt
½ teaspoon freshly ground black pepper

In a small saucepan, melt the butter over moderate heat; add the garlic, onion, and celery, and cook, while stirring, for 3 minutes. Stir in the flour and cook another minute before adding the milk, cream, and chopped cilantro. Bring the mixture to a boil, simmer gently for 10 minutes, then remove from heat.

In a blender or food processor, purée the soup until smooth, return mixture to the saucepan, bring back to a boil, season with salt and pepper, and serve.

SERVES 4

People either love or hate cilantro. This soup manages to win converts over to the love side; but if you believe nothing in the world will get you to like cilantro, leave it out, increase the amount of garlic to nine cloves, and enjoy cream of garlic soup!

MEXICAN TORTILLA SOUP

There are as many variations on this soup as there are cooks. Some manage to be better than others, but they all seem to be good—in fact, good enough that you can make a meal of it. Personalize this soup by varying the vegetables, but be sure to retain the spices and the tortilla and avocado garnish.

1 cup fresh corn kernels
2 tablespoons sweet butter
4 cloves garlic, minced
1 cup onion, diced
1 cup celery, diced
½ cup carrots, diced
½ cup Anaheim chile, seeded and diced
    (see directions on page xix)
1 tablespoon ground cumin
1½ tablespoons chile powder
1 teaspoon dried oregano
1½ cups tomatoes, diced
1 quart (4 cups) chicken stock or water
1 bunch cilantro, chopped
1½ cups cooked chicken, diced
1½ tablespoons coarse salt
½ teaspoon freshly ground black pepper
2 cups tortilla chips, broken into smaller pieces
1 avocado, diced
1 cup Monterey Jack cheese, grated

Cut raw kernels off corn cob with a sharp knife. In a large saucepan, melt the butter over moderate heat, add the garlic, onion, celery, corn, carrots, and chile and cook for 3 minutes, stirring occasionally, until the onion is translucent. Stir in the cumin, chile powder, and oregano and continue stirring another minute to toast the spices. Add the tomatoes, stock, cilantro, and chicken, bring mixture to a boil, and simmer for 10 minutes. Season with salt and pepper.

To serve, distribute the broken tortilla chips equally in the bottom of soup bowls, ladle the soup over them, and garnish each bowl with a tablespoon each of the diced avocado and the cheese.

SERVES 8–10

RED CHILE CORN CHOWDER

3 cups fresh corn kernels
2 tablespoons sweet butter
4 cloves garlic, minced
2 cups onion, diced
1 cup celery, diced
1 cup red bell pepper, diced
½ cup Anaheim chile, seeded and diced
    (see directions on page xix)
2 tablespoons chile powder
¼ cup flour
4 cups milk
1 cup heavy cream
2 tablespoons coarse salt

The addition of chile powder to this, otherwise, basic corn chowder recipe, adds a whole new dimension. Substitute frozen corn if you must, but this soup is at its best when fresh corn is used at its sweetest. If you're shy on spice, you may want to adjust the heat by changing the amount or variety of chile powder.

Cut raw kernels off corn cob with a sharp knife. In a large saucepan, melt the butter over moderate heat; then, add the garlic, onion, celery, red peppers, Anaheim chile, and corn. Cook, stirring occasionally, for 4 minutes. Stir in the chile powder and flour and cook another minute. Add the milk and cream, bring mixture to a boil, and simmer gently for 5 minutes. Season with salt and serve.

SERVES 6

SWEET GREEN SALAD WITH LEMON GRASS VINAIGRETTE

There's nothing more refreshing than a simple green salad to precede or follow an entrée. This salad, which makes use of the mellow flavor of lemon grass, is a perfect example of how good simplicity can be.

LEMON GRASS VINAIGRETTE

1 cup seasoned rice wine vinegar
1 stalk lemon grass, chopped
1 tablespoon sugar
1 small shallot, minced
1 teaspoon fresh tarragon, chopped
1 cup peanut oil
1 tablespoon sesame oil

1 large bowl assorted salad greens

Combine the rice wine vinegar and lemon grass in a small saucepan and bring to a boil over low heat. Remove from heat and allow to cool. Strain the lemon grass from the vinegar. Place the vinegar in a mixing bowl with the sugar, shallot, and tarragon and whisk in the oils slowly until combined.

Toss with the dressing and serve the salad greens.

SERVES 4

SMOKED SALMON JERKY CAESAR SALAD

DRESSING

2 ounces smoked salmon jerky
1 clove garlic
1 tablespoon grain mustard
1 tablespoon Worcestershire sauce
1 tablespoon capers
¼ cup sun-dried tomatoes
1 shallot, chopped
¼ cup red wine vinegar
1¼ cups olive oil
½ teaspoon freshly ground black pepper

1 head romaine lettuce
½ cup freshly grated Romano cheese
1 cup croutons, freshly toasted (see directions
*   on page xviii)*

To make the dressing, combine smoked salmon jerky, garlic, mustard, Worcestershire sauce, capers, sun-dried tomatoes, and shallot. Pass through the fine blade of a meat grinder or process in a food processor. Remove mixture to a bowl, add the red wine vinegar, and whisk in the olive oil slowly. Season with the freshly ground black pepper.

Wash the lettuce, drain well, and cut into bite-sized pieces. Toss greens with Romano cheese; then, toss with the dressing. Garnish with croutons and serve.

SERVES 6

There's documented proof that the Caesar salad was created in Tijuana, Mexico, just seventeen miles from downtown San Diego. The Smoked Salmon Jerky Caesar was created when someone sent me a sample of salmon jerky. Fascinated by its intense flavor, I thought about what I might do with it, and for some reason, possibly its high salt content, it dawned on me that if I substituted salmon jerky for the anchovy in a caesar salad, I may never again have to respond to requests for a "caesar salad, hold the anchovy."

CAESAR SALAD WITH GRILLED STEAK

Though this Caesar dressing is more traditional than its smoked salmon jerky counterpart, there's nothing traditional about serving it with grilled steak, or, for that matter, with shrimp, fried oysters, or smoked chicken. Consider any, or all, these options when you want something more substantial than just greens.

DRESSING

4 egg yolks
2 tablespoons red wine vinegar
2 tablespoons fresh lemon juice
2 tablespoons anchovy paste or 4 anchovies, mashed into a paste
4 cloves garlic, minced
3 tablespoons Dijon mustard
1 tablespoon dry mustard
2 tablespoons freshly ground black pepper
1 tablespoon Worcestershire sauce
1 teaspoon sugar
2 cups olive oil

1 large head romaine lettuce, torn into bite-sized pieces
1 cup freshly grated Parmesan cheese
1 pound grilled steak, cold and sliced thinly
3 large beefsteak tomatoes, cut into wedges
2 cups croutons, freshly toasted (see directions on page xviii)

In a small mixing bowl, mix all the dressing ingredients together except the olive oil. Gradually, whisk in the oil in a steady stream until combined.

To assemble the salad, toss the lettuce, Parmesan cheese, sliced steak, and dressing in a large bowl until coated uniformly. Divide the mixture among 6 chilled plates. Garnish each salad with tomato wedges and toasted croutons and serve.

SERVES 6

VINE RIPE TOMATO AND CUCUMBER SALAD WITH RED BEAN VINAIGRETTE

RED BEAN VINAIGRETTE

⅔ cup Oriental sweet red bean paste
1 egg yolk
2 teaspoons chile and garlic paste
⅔ cup rice wine vinegar
1⅓ cup peanut oil
1 tablespoon sesame oil

3 cups cucumbers, peeled, seeded, and diced
8 large vine ripe tomatoes, cut into wedges
½ cup scallions, sliced thinly
3 tablespoons sesame seeds, toasted
(see directions on page xviii)

For the vinaigrette, combine the bean paste, egg yolk, chile and garlic paste, and rice wine vinegar in a bowl and whisk in the peanut and sesame oils gradually until combined.

To serve the salad, coat the entire surface of each plate generously with Red Bean Vinaigrette. Divide the diced cucumber equally and place a mound in the center of each plate. Arrange the tomato wedges around the cucumber center in a flower pattern. Sprinkle with scallions and toasted sesame seeds and serve.

SERVES 8

We received shipment of a case of Oriental sweet red bean paste at the restaurant by mistake, and because of some procrastination the time period during which it could be returned passed. While the bean paste is quite popular in certain Asian desserts, I had a hard time envisioning our patrons finishing off their meals with this sweet meat. It took some time and a lot of modifications, but the Red Bean Vinaigrette proved to be just the thing to pair with the full flavor of summer vine ripened tomatoes.

I managed to use up the entire case of red bean paste as was my objective, but, as popularity demanded, I had to order more.

SPINACH SALAD WITH GRILLED LAMB

VINAIGRETTE
1 large egg
¼ cup red wine vinegar
½ teaspoon ground cumin
½ cup cilantro, chopped
¼ teaspoon freshly ground black pepper
1 clove garlic, minced
1 tablespoon sugar
½ teaspoon coarse salt
⅔ cup peanut oil

2 quarts (8 cups) spinach, cleaned
1 cup red bell pepper, julienned
1 cup jicama, peeled and julienned
¼ cup pine nuts, toasted (see directions
*   on page xviii)*

To make the vinaigrette, place the egg in a blender or food processor along with the red wine vinegar, spices, herbs, sugar, and salt and process while adding the oil slowly until combined.

Place the spinach, lamb, pepper, and jicama in a large bowl, and toss with the vinaigrette. Garnish with the pine nuts and serve.

SERVES 4

SASHIMI AND FRUIT SALAD WITH PICKLED GINGER VINAIGRETTE

PICKLED GINGER VINAIGRETTE
¼ *cup sherry wine vinegar*
¼ *cup honey*
2 *teaspoons pickled ginger, minced*
¼ *cup sesame oil*
¼ *cup walnut oil*
2 *tablespoons sesame seeds, toasted*
  (see directions on page xviii)

¾ *pound sashimi-grade ahi, sliced*
1 *cup strawberries*
½ *small cantaloupe, peeled and sliced*
2 *small peaches, sliced*
½ *small honeydew melon, peeled and sliced*
1 *cup blueberries*
1 *cup raspberries*

When fish is impeccably fresh and fruit is truly ripe, I can think of no better union, especially when complemented with this nutty vinaigrette dipping sauce. Although I specify ahi as my fish of choice, don't hesitate to substitute your favorite fish.

To make the vinaigrette, combine the vinegar with the honey and pickled ginger in a small mixing bowl. Whisk in the sesame and walnut oils gradually until combined. Stir in the sesame seeds.

To serve, arrange the sliced ahi and fresh fruit attractively in a bowl and serve the vinaigrette as a dipping sauce for both.

SERVES 4

THAI CHICKEN SALAD WITH SPICY PEANUT VINAIGRETTE

For a while it seemed as though restaurants and their Chinese chicken salads were becoming as trendy as restaurants and cheesecakes. And everyone had the ultimate version. I finally refused to do another Chinese chicken salad with sesame dressing and opted instead for this Thai spiced salad with a peanut vinaigrette, which is every bit as popular as its predecessor. In the restaurant, we use a Thai black rice that is difficult to come by. If you have access to it, don't fail to avail yourself to its nutty quality.

SPICY PEANUT VINAIGRETTE

1/4 cup peanut butter
6 tablespoons Thai Marinade (page 7)
6 tablespoons rice wine vinegar
1/2 cup cilantro, chopped
3/4 cup peanut oil

1 cup Oriental short-grained rice, uncooked
1 cup broccoli florets
1 cup carrots, peeled and sliced
12 asparagus spears (3 inches long)
1 large red bell pepper, julienned
3/4 pound chicken breast, cooked and sliced
2 tablespoons Thai Marinade (page 7)
1/4 cup peanuts, chopped

For the peanut vinaigrette, place all ingredients except the peanut oil in a food processor or blender and process while adding the oil gradually, until combined.

Cook the rice according to package instructions; then, allow rice to cool to room temperature.

In a large saucepan of boiling water, blanch the broccoli for 1 minute. Quickly remove the broccoli from the hot water and immerse in ice water to stop it from cooking further. Repeat this procedure with the carrots and asparagus (leave red pepper raw). Drain all the vegetables and pat dry with a towel.

In a small bowl, toss the sliced chicken in the Thai Marinade and allow it to sit in the liquid for 5–10 minutes until you are ready to assemble.

To assemble the salad, divide the rice among four plates. Divide and arrange the vegetables and chicken around the rice. Drizzle the vinaigrette over all and garnish plates with the chopped peanuts.

SERVES 4

Shrimp with Three-Tomato Chile (recipe on page 102) ⇒

GRILLED CHICKEN SALAD WITH RED PEPPER RAJAS AND BLUE CHEESE VINAIGRETTE

BLUE CHEESE VINAIGRETTE

6 tablespoons balsamic vinegar
1 tablespoon dried oregano
1 tablespoon dried basil
2 teaspoons sugar
1 teaspoon dry mustard
½ cup olive oil
8 ounces blue cheese, crumbled

1 large bowl assorted salad greens
1½ pounds grilled chicken meat, cut into strips
2 recipes Red Pepper Rajas (page 134)
2 cups tortilla chips

For the vinaigrette, combine the vinegar, oregano, basil, sugar, and dry mustard in a bowl and whisk in the olive oil slowly until combined. Stir in the blue cheese crumbles gently.

To assemble the salad, toss the salad greens with the blue cheese vinaigrette in a large bowl. Divide the greens among 6 plates. Garnish each salad with an equal amount of grilled chicken strips, drained Red Pepper Rajas, and tortilla chips and serve.

SERVES 6

If it isn't Chinese chicken salad and you want to sell it, better serve it with blue cheese dressing! This blue cheese dressing is a light vinaigrette, not the creamy variety, which makes it okay if you're watching your diet.

⇐ *Clockwise from top: Gazpacho Gold (recipe on page 57), Mexican Tortilla Soup (recipe on page 62), Japanese Clam and Water Chestnut Chowder (recipe on page 60)*

AVOCADO AND RADICCHIO SALAD WITH MANGO VINAIGRETTE

This colorful salad is rich and soothing. The sweetness of ripe mango is tempered in the vinaigrette and provides a spectacular contrast to the creamy, nutlike quality of ripe avocados, as well as to the bitterness of radicchio.

MANGO VINAIGRETTE
2 cups mango, peeled and diced
¼ cup rice wine vinegar
1 teaspoon honey
¼ teaspoon chile powder
¼ teaspoon freshly ground black pepper
¼ cup sesame oil

2 large ripe avocados
4 large radicchio leaves
2 tablespoons cilantro, chopped

For the vinaigrette, combine the mango, rice wine vinegar, honey, chile powder, and pepper in a blender or food processor, and process while adding the oil gradually, until smooth. If mixture is too thick, adjust by adding water, but additional honey may be needed to retain the level of flavor.

To assemble the salad, halve, seed, and peel the avocados. On each plate, place a radicchio leaf and center an avocado half on top. Generously ladle dressing over the avocado and onto the plate. Garnish with chopped cilantro.

SERVES 4

SPAGHETTI WESTERNS

Long before Italians began copying Hollywood cowboy epics, Marco Polo returned from his journey to China and introduced pasta to Italy for one of the most popular remakes in history! No wonder, as pasta is comforting, filling, and even healthy, as well as providing the perfect vehicle for your favorite sauce.

One of the things I enjoy most about creating pasta dishes is the freedom it gives me to match food trends with the wide assortment of pasta varieties and shapes, as the following recipes will demonstrate. For your own creations, try substituting different shapes of pasta for those I've suggested. Toss your favorite pasta adventures with some of the salsa or soup recipes. I particularly recommend pasta with the Spicy Oriental Black Bean Salsa and the Red Chile Corn Chowder.

LINGUINI WITH WILD MUSHROOMS

This is our rendition of pasta primavera, one of this century's most popular noodle creations in which pasta provides a perfect backdrop for garlic and a melange of fresh spring vegetables. You may find debate among chefs as to whether it should be made with a cream sauce or olive oil. We subscribe to the olive oil, which produces a lighter and healthier dish. If you cannot obtain wild mushrooms in your market, substitute fresh domestic mushrooms. For those of you who are true garlic lovers, don't hesitate to increase the quantity suggested here in proportion to your love of the wonderful *stinking rose*.

¾ cup olive oil
6 cloves garlic, minced
2 cups fresh wild mushrooms, sliced
1 can (8½ ounces drained weight) unmarinated
    artichoke hearts, quartered
½ cup scallions, sliced thinly
½ cup sun-dried tomatoes, diced
12 ounces fresh linguini, cooked and drained
2 tablespoons coarse salt
½ teaspoon freshly ground black pepper
1 cup freshly grated Parmesan cheese

Heat ¼ cup of the olive oil in a large skillet over moderate heat. Add the garlic and cook for 30 seconds; then, add the wild mushrooms, artichokes hearts, scallions, and sun-dried tomatoes. Stir while cooking for approximately 2 minutes, until the mushrooms soften.

Toss in the linguini, add the remaining ½ cup olive oil, season with salt and pepper, and remove from heat. Garnish with Parmesan cheese and serve immediately.

SERVES 4

THE BLT (BACON, LINGUINI, AND TOMATO)

8 slices smoked bacon, diced
3 cloves garlic, minced
12 ounces fresh linguini, cooked and drained
2 tablespoons coarse salt
½ teaspoon freshly ground black pepper
2 cups tomatoes, diced
1 bunch cilantro, chopped
1 cup freshly grated Parmesan cheese

In a large skillet over moderate heat, cook the diced bacon until the fat is rendered and the bacon is crisp. Stir in the garlic and cook for 30 seconds or so to cook out the raw taste; then, toss in the cooked linguini.

Season the linguini with salt and pepper, remove from the heat, and toss in the tomatoes and cilantro. Garnish with Parmesan cheese and serve immediately.

SERVES 4

There's no bread in this BLT! The key to this dish is selecting a good, smoky bacon. If bacon's not in your diet, substitute one-fourth cup of olive oil as your cooking fat and toss in one cup of your favorite smoked meat, thinly sliced and julienned, when you add the tomatoes and cilantro.

CHINESE CHICKEN RAVIOLI

In the restaurant, this is our designer ravioli. Not only are they distinguished by their fire-cracker shape, but we also use a red and black striped pasta dough that is made specially for us by one of our purveyors. If you're able to buy fresh pasta dough, though you may not find it striped, try to get a variety of colors to create an equally graphic effect.

3 tablespoons peanut oil
4 cloves garlic, minced
1 teaspoon fresh ginger, minced
2 cups shiitake mushrooms, stemmed and sliced
¼ cup Teriyaki Sauce (page 7)
1 teaspoon chile and garlic paste
¾ pound chicken breast, skinless and boneless
5 egg whites
2 teaspoons sesame oil
1 large red bell pepper, diced
½ cup cilantro, chopped
¾ pound smoked chicken, diced
1 pound fresh pasta dough
1 recipe Oriental Mustard Salsa (page 9)

Heat peanut oil in a large skillet over moderate heat; then, add the garlic and ginger and cook for 1 minute. Stir in the sliced mushrooms, cook an additional minute and add the Teriyaki Sauce. Over high heat, continue cooking until almost all the liquid has evaporated. Remove from heat, stir in the chile and garlic paste, and allow mixture to cool.

Chop the chicken breast roughly and place in a food processor along with 1 of the egg whites and the sesame oil. Process until mixture is smooth.

In a large bowl, combine the processed chicken, cooled mushroom mixture, red bell pepper, cilantro, and smoked chicken and mix until combined evenly.

To make the ravioli, cut the pasta dough into 2½ × 5-inch rectangles, brush the entire surface with remaining egg white, and place a ½-inch tube of filling lengthwise in the center of each rectangle, leaving a 1-inch border on each end. Roll the dough around the filling to create a cylinder-shaped ravioli, pinching each end firmly where the filling ends to seal. Repeat this procedure until all ravioli are made.

To cook, place the ravioli in a large pot of boiling water and cook over high heat for approximately 4 minutes, or when ravioli is firm to the touch. Drain and serve with warmed Oriental Mustard Salsa.

SERVES 4

KUNG PAO CALAMARI WITH JAPANESE SOBA NOODLES

2 tablespoons peanut oil
2 cloves garlic, minced
1/2 cup red bell pepper, julienned
3/4 pound calamari, cleaned (see directions
      on page xix)
1/2 cup unsalted peanuts
1 recipe Kung Pao Sauce
12 ounces soba noodles, cooked and drained
1/2 cup scallions, sliced thinly

In a wok or skillet, heat the peanut oil over high heat. When hot, add in quick succession the garlic, the red pepper, and the calamari and peanuts, stirring all ingredients rapidly. After cooking the calamari for 30 seconds, add the Kung Pao Sauce and, last, add the noodles, tossing to combine all ingredients. Remove from heat immediately, garnish with sliced scallions, and serve.

SERVES 4

People in San Diego always seem to be in search of the ultimate kung pao in Chinese restaurants. My version of the sauce is anything but authentic because it includes the addition of hoisin, or Chinese barbeque sauce, but it makes a wonderful sweet and spicy sauce for this dish and for stir-fries of all kinds.

Normally kung pao is served with rice, but one day I didn't want to take the time, so I quickly cooked some soba noodles, an ingredient that has remained part of this dish ever since.

KUNG PAO SAUCE

1/2 cup hoisin sauce
1/2 cup Teriyaki Sauce (page 7)
1/2 cup plus 2 tablespoons cold water
2 tablespoons sherry wine vinegar
1 pod star anise
1 tablespoon chile and garlic paste
2 tablespoons cornstarch

Combine all ingredients, except the cornstarch and two tablespoons of cold water, in a small saucepan. Over low heat, bring to a boil. Simmer 10 minutes.

Dissolve cornstarch in the remaining cold water and whisk into the mixture, bring back to a boil, and remove from heat.

MAKES 1 3/4 CUPS

SPINACH PAPPARDELLE WITH SEA SCALLOPS AND JALAPÉNO CREAM

This was the very first south-western pasta to appear on our menu and has remained an extremely popular dish. The heat of jalapeño pepper is soothed by the sweetness of scallops, the touch of lime juice, and the neutrality of the noodles and cream.

Pappardelle is a wide, flat noodle. But as with any pasta dish, choose the shape of noodle you like best.

6 tablespoons (¾ stick) sweet butter
2 cloves garlic, minced
1 small jalapeño pepper, seeded and minced
   (see directions on page xix)
1 pound fresh sea scallops
¼ cup dry vermouth
3 cups heavy cream
1 tablespoon coarse salt
¼ teaspoon freshly ground black pepper
2 tablespoons fresh lime juice
12 ounces fresh spinach pappardelle, cooked
   and drained
2 small red bell peppers, julienned

Melt 3 tablespoons of the butter in a large skillet over moderate heat. Add the garlic and minced jalapeño pepper, cook for 1 minute; then, add the scallops and cook for appoximately 3 minutes while stirring occasionally.

Raise the heat to high and add the vermouth, allowing it to cook until only a tablespoon of liquid is left; add the cream, salt and pepper, and the remaining 3 tablespoons butter and boil until the sauce begins to thicken. Add the lime juice, toss in the pasta, garnish with the julienne of red peppers, and serve.

SERVES 4

PENNE WITH CHICKEN AND TOASTED PECANS

18 tablespoons (2 1/4 sticks) sweet butter, room
*   temperature*
1/2 cup pecans, toasted and chopped finely
*   (see directions on page xviii)*
2 large egg yolks
2 cloves garlic, minced
1 tablespoon heavy cream
1 tablespoon coarse salt
1 teaspoon freshly ground black pepper
4 ounces goat cheese, soft
3/4 pound chicken breast, skinless, boneless, and
*   cut into 1/2-inch strips*
12 ounces dried penne, cooked and drained

In a bowl, mix 1 cup (2 sticks) of the butter with the pecans, egg yolks, garlic, cream, salt, pepper, and goat cheese until well blended.

Melt the remaining 2 tablespoons butter, in a large skillet over moderate heat. Add the chicken strips and cook for 4–5 minutes until the chicken is almost done. Reduce heat and add the pecan butter mixture, stirring until the mixture melts and takes on a saucelike appearance. Toss in the cooked penne and serve.

SERVES 4

This is an extremely rich and satisfying preparation, which, in small portions, makes an excellent starter. The flavor that the toasted pecans adds is particularly striking and is a perfect foil for the goat cheese. If another type of nut is more appealing to you, don't hesitate to substitute.

GRILLED SWORDFISH AND RIGATONI WITH TOMATO, BASIL, AND ALMOND SALSA

Rigatoni is one of those pasta shapes that seems to be associated with heavy, old-fashioned dishes. This recipe proves that association to be untrue. If shark is more available and affordable than swordfish, don't hesitate to substitute.

The salsa recipe originated deep in the heart of Sicily. It's actually a pesto in which basil is delegated to a secondary role. The use of toasted almonds, as well as the addition of fresh tomatoes, lends a wonderful flavor.

1 1/2 pounds swordfish, cubed and skewered
1/2 cup olive oil
3 cloves garlic, minced
1/2 teaspoon freshly ground black pepper
1 recipe Tomato, Basil, and Almond Salsa
2 tablespoons coarse salt
12 ounces dried rigatoni, cooked and drained

Marinate the swordfish in the olive oil, garlic, and black pepper mixture for at least 1 hour before grilling. If the salsa has been refrigerated, remove so it will be at room temperature when added.

When ready to grill, season the swordfish with salt and cook over hot coals approximately 4–5 minutes, slightly longer than 2 minutes on each side.

Toss the rigatoni in a bowl with the salsa, stirring well to coat the pasta. Remove the grilled swordfish from the skewers and serve on top of the rigatoni.

SERVES 4

TOMATO, BASIL, AND ALMOND SALSA

½ cup blanched almonds, toasted (see directions
     on page xviii)
3 cloves garlic
1½ cups fresh basil leaves
1 small jalapeño pepper, seeded (see directions
     on page xix)
½ cup olive oil
1 teaspoon fresh lime juice
2 cups tomatoes, diced
1 tablespoon coarse salt
⅛ teaspoon freshly ground black pepper

In a blender or food processor, combine the almonds, garlic, basil, and jalapeño pepper. Process while adding the olive oil and lime juice gradually. When mixture is almost smooth, remove to a small bowl and mix in the tomatoes, salt, and pepper. Serve at room temperature. This pesto is best when used the same day it is prepared.

MAKES 3 CUPS

LINGUINI AND SWEET CRAB WITH GOLDEN TOMATO CURRY SAUCE

I always seem to get pleasing results when I substitute pasta in dishes where rice was called for originally. I haven't yet tried the reverse, using rice for traditionally pasta dishes, but it does raise numerous possibilities.

I find that most people are afraid of curry, and I probably should have changed the name of the sauce used in this dish to Golden Tomato Salsa to alleviate that fear. But, really, this is user-friendly curry. You'll find the sauce equally appealing with grilled lamb and chicken dishes. If golden tomatoes aren't available, go ahead and substitute six cups of chopped red tomatoes.

2 tablespoons sweet butter
1 cup onion, sliced
2 cloves garlic, minced
1 cup red bell pepper, julienned
1 pound lump crabmeat, cleaned and cooked
1 bunch cilantro, chopped
12 ounces fresh linguini, cooked and drained
1 recipe Golden Tomato Curry Sauce

Melt the butter in a large skillet over moderate heat, add the onion, garlic, and red bell peppers and cook briefly, until just slightly softened. Quickly, toss in the crabmeat, cilantro, and linguini; then, toss with the Golden Tomato Curry Sauce; and serve.

SERVES 4

GOLDEN TOMATO CURRY SAUCE

1½ tablespoons olive oil
1 clove garlic, minced
½ cup leeks, diced
2 tablespoons curry powder
2 pints fresh yellow pear tomatoes
1 can (14 ounces) coconut milk
1 tablespoon honey
1½ teaspoons brown sugar
1½ teaspoons coarse salt

In a small saucepan, heat the olive oil over moderate heat; add the garlic and leeks and cook gently for 2–3 minutes. Stir in the curry, and continuing to stir the mixture, cook another minute before adding the tomatoes, coconut milk, honey, and brown sugar. Bring the sauce to a simmer and cook for 20 minutes.

Place sauce in a blender or food processor and purée. Strain the mixture well. Return mixture to saucepan, bring back to a simmer, and season with salt. Serve warm.

MAKES 3 CUPS

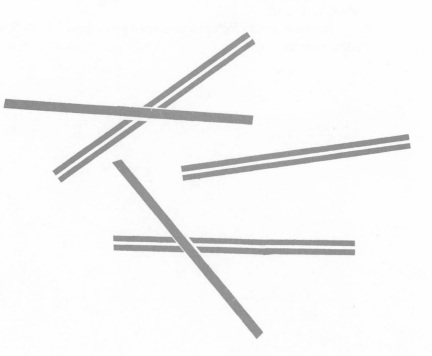

SPICY SEAFOOD FETTUCCINI

~~~~~~~~~~~~~~~~~~~~~~~~~~~~~~~~

Andrew Schneider, who
worked as chef in the kitchens
of Cafe Pacifica for several
years, added this dish to our
menu, which was immediately
dubbed "for garlic lovers
only."

3 tablespoons olive oil
2 cloves garlic, minced
½ pound swordfish, diced into 1-inch cubes
¼ pound bay scallops
18 large shrimp, peeled and deveined
   (see directions on page xix)
2 large red bell peppers, julienned
½ cup scallions, sliced thinly
¾ teaspoon coarse salt
½ teaspoon onion powder
¼ teaspoon cayenne pepper
½ teaspoon Spanish paprika
½ teaspoon dried thyme leaves
¼ teaspoon freshly ground black pepper
1 cup tomatoes, diced
½ cup fish stock
6 tablespoons (¾ stick) sweet butter
1 pound fresh fettuccini, cooked and drained

Heat the olive oil in a skillet over moderate heat. Add the garlic and cook for 30 seconds; then, add the seafood and cook, while stirring, for another minute. Add the red peppers, scallions, and seasonings. Cook for 1 minute and add the tomatoes, fish stock, and butter.

Increase heat to high and cook until sauce begins to thicken. Serve over the fettuccini.

SERVES 6

GORGONZOLA RAVIOLI WITH SWEET RED PEPPER CREAM

RAVIOLI

8 ounces ricotta cheese
8 ounces Gorgonzola cheese
¼ cup pine nuts, toasted (page xviii)
1 tablespoon fresh basil, chopped
1 teaspoon fresh oregano, chopped
1 tablespoon coarse salt
½ teaspoon freshly ground black pepper
1 pound fresh pasta sheets
2 egg whites

SWEET RED PEPPER CREAM

2 tablespoons sweet butter
2 cloves garlic, minced
3 large red bell peppers, roasted, peeled, and
  diced (see directions on page xix)
2 tablespoons flour
1½ cups milk
½ cup heavy cream
2 teaspoons coarse salt
¼ teaspoon freshly ground black pepper

This cheese ravioli was first introduced to us by our good friends and neighbors, Roberto and Luigi Assenti of the Assenti Pasta Company. When I have a burst of energy, I make my own, using the following recipe which varies from the Assenti's mostly by the addition of pine nuts. As with all dishes, the better the ingredients, the better the finished product. Use imported Gorgonzola!

To make the ravioli, thoroughly mix the cheeses with the pine nuts, fresh herbs, salt, and pepper. From the pasta dough, cut twenty-four 3-inch circles. Brush each circle with egg white and distribute the filling evenly, placing it in the center of each circle. Fold circle in half to enclose the filling and create a half-moon shape. Make sure edges are pressed together and sealed tightly.

For the sauce, melt butter over moderate heat in a small saucepan, add the garlic and diced peppers, and continue to cook for a minute or so. Stir in the flour and cook an additional minute before adding the milk and cream. Bring the mixture to a boil, then, reduce the heat and simmer gently for 5 minutes. Purée the sauce in a blender or food processor, return to the saucepan, bring the mixture back to a simmer, and season with salt and pepper.

When ready, cook the ravioli for 2–3 minutes in a large pot of boiling salted water. Drain, pour sauce on plates and serve ravioli on top of the sauce.

SERVES 4

LARGE PLATES

Large Plates is the term we use for the main course, or entrée selections, and reflects not merely quantity, but the search for flavor combinations that become more and more desirable with each bite. Unlike Small Plates, which are teasers meant to wake up your taste buds and appetite, Large Plates are meant to satisfy and warm the soul. Don't wait for company to prepare them. The following creations are so special you'll want to share them with your family.

MUSTARD CATFISH

MARINADE

1 cup prepared mustard
2 cups Dijon mustard
2 tablespoons chile powder
1 tablespoon dried thyme leaves
1 tablespoon Spanish paprika
1 tablespoon dried oregano
2 cloves garlic, minced
2 tablespoons freshly ground black pepper
1 tablespoon coarse salt
2 tablespoons fresh lemon juice

6 catfish fillets ($\frac{1}{2}$ pound each)
4 cups Ritz cracker crumbs, coarse
4 tablespoons ($\frac{1}{2}$ stick) sweet butter
1 recipe Jalapeño Tartar Sauce (page 17)

For the Marinade, simply mix all the ingredients together in a bowl. Marinate the fillets in this mixture overnight, or at least 8 hours prior to cooking.

Preheat a griddle or warm a skillet over moderate heat. Roll the mustard-coated catfish fillets in the cracker crumbs so both sides of the fish are completely covered. Melt butter on the griddle and cook the fish approximately 3–4 minutes per side, until crust is golden brown. Serve with Jalapeño Tartar Sauce.

SERVES 6

WOK-CHARRED CATFISH WITH SPICY ORIENTAL BLACK BEAN SALSA

BLACKENING SEASONING

½ cup sugar
1½ teaspoon dry mustard
¼ teaspoon ground cinnamon
2 tablespoons dried oregano leaves
1 teaspoon dried thyme leaves
1 tablespoon Spanish paprika
1 tablespoon cocoa
⅔ cup chili powder
2 tablespoons ground cumin
2 tablespoons freshly ground black pepper
¼ cup coarse salt
1 cup sesame seeds, toasted (see directions
on page xviii)

8 catfish fillets (½ pound each)
3 tablespoons peanut oil
1 recipe Spicy Oriental Black Bean Salsa
(page 8)

For the Blackening Seasoning, combine all ingredients together in a bowl. Just before cooking, roll the catfish fillets in spice mixture so fillets are coated generously.

Preheat a wok or cast-iron skillet over moderately high heat, add the peanut oil, and when it starts to smoke, add the catfish fillets and cook for approximately 3 minutes on each side. Serve with warm Spicy Oriental Black Bean Salsa.

SERVES 8

Most versions of catfish with black bean sauce use the whole fish, including the head. Our patrons in San Diego simply weren't ready for their dinner to stare them in the face, so I created this dish with catfish fillets, making up in spice what it lost in presentation.

YUCATAN BARBEQUED
KING SALMON

Achiote paste is the Yucatan spice most often associated with pork pibil, a well-known Mexican dish. I tried using this recipe's marinade on a number of fish similar to those used in Mexican cooking, but, I must admit, with unsatisfying results. When I finally tried it with salmon, I knew I'd found a true match, especially when it was voted Best Seafood Dish of 1988 by *San Diego Union* food editor, Maureen Clancey.

12 ounces achiote paste
2 cups orange juice
6 salmon fillets (7 ounces each)
6 wedges lime

Crumble achiote paste into the orange juice and mix until completely dissolved. Marinate the salmon in this mixture overnight, or at least 4 hours before grilling.

Cook salmon over a hot grill until medium rare, 2 minutes on each side, and serve with lime wedges.

SERVES 6

SUGAR-SPICED BARBEQUED KING SALMON WITH CHINESE HOT MUSTARD

SUGAR-SPICE COATING

½ cup sugar
1 teaspoon dry mustard
¼ teaspoon ground cinnamon
1 tablespoon Spanish paprika
2 teaspoons cocoa
½ cup chili powder
2 tablespoons ground cumin
1 tablespoon freshly ground black pepper
¼ cup coarse salt

6 salmon fillets (7 ounces each)
1 recipe Chinese Hot Mustard (page 9)

For the Sugar-Spice Coating simply combine all ingredients in a bowl. Just before grilling, roll the salmon fillets in the mixture so they are coated generously. Place on a hot grill and cook until salmon is medium rare, 2–3 minutes on each side. Remove and serve with Chinese Hot Mustard.

SERVES 6

This recipe, in which salmon is coated with a variety of spices, originated from the concept of blackened fish that Paul Prudhomme has made so popular. The spices I use are for flavor more than fire, but use caution with the Chinese Hot Mustard!

POACHED SALMON WITH ROASTED RED PEPPER AND DILL SALSA

The origin of this recipe is New York City's acclaimed Quilted Giraffe where I worked as sous-chef. There, we gently poached fresh salmon in the salsa and, when it was served, adorned the fish with the salsa's fresh solids. This dish still ranks as one of my all-time favorites, not just to prepare, but to eat.

1 recipe Roasted Red Pepper and Dill Salsa
6 salmon fillets (7 ounces each)

The salsa should be at room temperature; divide the mixture in half. Warm half of the salsa in a sauté pan over very low heat. When warm, place the salmon fillets in the pan with the salsa, cover, and continue cooking over low heat for 4–5 minutes, or until the salmon is medium rare.

Remove salmon from pan, drain the excess poaching salsa, and serve, topped with the reserved heated salsa.

SERVES 6

ROASTED RED PEPPER AND DILL SALSA

5 large red bell peppers, roasted, peeled, and
*   cut into a ½-inch dice (see directions*
*   on page xix)*
1 clove garlic, minced
1 head shallot minced
1 cup cilantro, chopped coarsely
2 cups dill, chopped coarsely
1 cup tomatoes, diced
⅓ cup white wine vinegar
½ cup olive oil
¼ cup walnut oil
¼ cup sesame oil
2 tablespoons white port
1½ tablespoons coarse salt
½ teaspoon freshly ground black pepper

Combine peppers in a bowl with the garlic, shallot, cilantro, dill, and tomatoes.

While stirring, slowly add vinegar, the oils, and the port. Season with salt and pepper. Mixture should stand 1 hour at room temperature before serving. Best used the same day.

MAKES 6 CUPS

GRILLED KING SALMON WITH PLUM-PEPPER SAUCE

2 teaspoons Chinese five spice
¼ cup peanut oil
6 salmon fillets (½ pound each)
1 cup Chinese plum sauce
2 tablespoons pickapepper sauce
1 tablespoon rice wine vinegar

Combine Chinese five spice with peanut oil and marinate salmon in this mixture for half an hour before cooking.

In a small saucepan over low heat, combine the plum sauce, pickapepper sauce, and rice wine vinegar.

Grill the salmon over a hot fire until medium rare, 2–3 minutes on each side. Serve immediately with the warm sauce.

SERVES 6

This is another creation of Andrew Schneider, the former chef at Cafe Pacifica in San Diego. At first, its ingredients seem a bit exotic. But if you look carefully, you'll probably be able to find everything you need at your market. It's almost too easy, and too good, to be true.

GRILLED HAWAIIAN AHI
WITH THAI FLAVORS

Ahi is the Hawaiian name for yellowfin tuna. One variety of tuna is not necessarily better than another, but there are definite differences in flavor, texture, and oil content. Ahi is popular because of its mild flavor. Make sure you request sashimi-quality tuna, whatever variety is available to you. My recipes suggest cooking ahi rare to medium rare to enjoy the optimal flavor. Strangely, it's only when you fully cook tuna that it becomes fishy tasting like canned tuna.

〜〜〜〜〜〜〜〜〜〜〜〜

From time to time, Pacifica Grill does joint functions with one of our neighboring restaurants, a fine steak house. For hors d'oeuvres, they often serve miniature prime rib sandwiches, and we serve rare ahi on toast with horseradish cream. It's amazing how many people think we, too, are serving beef. As the following recipe will attest, the flavor of ahi, like beef, stands up to strong spices.

2 cloves garlic, minced
1 teaspoon fresh mint, minced
2 cloves shallot, minced
2 tablespoons sesame seeds, toasted
   (see directions on page xviii)
3 tablespoons cilantro, chopped
2 tablespoons white wine
2 tablespoons rice wine vinegar
1 cup beef or chicken stock
1 cup Thai Marinade (page 7)
2 tablespoons sweet butter, cold
4 Hawaiian ahi steaks (7 ounces each)
2 tablespoons peanut oil
1 tablespoon coarse salt
½ teaspoon freshly ground black pepper

In a small saucepan over low heat, combine the garlic, mint, shallot, sesame seeds, cilantro, wine, and vinegar and cook until almost all the liquid is gone. Add the stock and Thai Marinade, bring to a boil, and simmer for 10 minutes. When ready to serve, remove from the heat and stir in the cold butter until it's completely incorporated into the sauce.

Brush the ahi steaks with peanut oil and season with salt and pepper. For medium rare steaks, grill over hot coals about 2 minutes on each side (for 1-inch thick steaks). Place ahi on a pool of sauce and serve.

SERVES 4

SEARED HAWAIIAN AHI WITH WILD MUSHROOM AND GINGER BUTTER

4 Hawaiian ahi steaks (6 ounces each)
1 tablespoon freshly ground black pepper
2 tablespoons coarse salt
2 tablespoons peanut oil
1 recipe Wild Mushroom and Ginger Butter

Season the ahi steaks generously with pepper and salt. Over high heat, in a sauté pan large enough to accommodate the ahi, heat the peanut oil until it begins to smoke. Carefully, place ahi in the pan and sear, 1 minute on each side for 1-inch steaks. Remove from pan and serve the steaks on a bed of Wild Mushroom and Ginger Butter.

SERVES 4

There's something special about fresh tuna, but the real secret here is the sauce. Try it on grilled steak or chicken, and even fresh pasta, too.

This large plate has been on our menu almost since the restaurant's inception. Considering the menu is printed on the computer daily, and my predisposition to change, that's an accomplishment for any dish.

WILD MUSHROOM AND GINGER BUTTER

8 tablespoons (1 stick) sweet butter
2 small cloves garlic, minced
½ teaspoon fresh ginger, minced
1 cup shiitake mushrooms, sliced
3 tablespoons scallions, sliced thinly
2 tablespoons Teriyaki Sauce (page 7)
2 tablespoons heavy cream

In a small saucepan over moderate heat, melt half the butter. Add the garlic and ginger and cook over low heat for 1 minute; add the mushrooms and scallions, cook for an additional minute. Then, increasing to high heat, add the Teriyaki Sauce, cream, and the remaining butter. Stir the mixture and continue cooking until sauce coats a spoon lightly. Remove from heat and serve immediately.

MAKES 1 CUP

WASABI-CRUSTED GRILLED HAWAIIAN AHI

The meatlike quality of Ahi is a perfect foil for the buttery crust that is flavored with wasabi, Japanese horseradish, and a hint of soy.

1½ teaspoons wasabi powder
1 tablespoon water
1 cup (2 sticks) sweet butter, room temperature
1 cup scallions, sliced thinly
2 cloves garlic, minced
¼ cup horseradish
1 tablespoon grain mustard
1 teaspoon sugar
1 egg yolk
½ cup panko bread crumbs
4 Hawaiian ahi steaks (6 ounces each)
½ cup Teriyaki Sauce (page 7)

Preheat broiler. In a mixing bowl, combine the wasabi powder and water and mix until a paste is formed. Add the butter, scallions, garlic, horseradish, mustard, sugar, egg yolk, and bread crumbs and mix until well combined. Set aside.

Grill ahi over the hottest area of the coals, basting frequently with Teriyaki Sauce, for approximately 2 minutes on each side. Remove from the grill, place ahi on a broiler pan, and spread the wasabi butter mixture evenly over the top of the fish. Place in broiler for 2–3 minutes, until the crust begins to brown lightly. Serve immediately.

SERVES 4

GRILLED TARE-GLAZED SWORDFISH WITH CHINESE PESTO

SWEET SOY GLAZE

½ cup soy sauce
⅜ cup mirin
¼ cup sugar

6 swordfish steaks (½ pound each)
1 recipe Chinese Pesto (page 19)

To prepare glaze, place all ingredients in a small saucepan and bring to a boil. Reduce heat and simmer until liquid is reduced to ½ cup. Allow glaze to cool before using.

Over a hot grill cook swordfish steaks, basting frequently with Sweet Soy Glaze, for approximately 2–3 minutes on each side for 1-inch-thick steaks. Serve with Chinese Pesto.

SERVES 6

If you frequent sushi bars, tare is the glaze often put on smoked eel. Wonderfully sweet, tare provides a good contrast to the steak-like quality of swordfish and a nice change of pace from teriyaki-marinated fish.

Mirin, sweet rice cooking wine, can be found in the Oriental section of many supermarkets, as well as in Oriental specialty stores.

SWORDFISH STEAK ASADA WITH TEQUILA AND SUN-DRIED TOMATO SALSA

In Mexico, you're likely to find *carne asada*, beef, or *pollo asada*, chicken, on the menu. Swordfish asada may eventually make it down that way, judging by its popularity on my menu. This preparation lends itself well to most steak fish, and it's pretty good with just plain beef steak, too. The salsa served on the swordfish is spicy and has great kick! There's nothing more natural than the combination of tequila and salsa. We've always paired it with this dish, but toss it with salad greens and freshly grated cheese and you'll put an end to dull salads.

1/2 cup olive oil
4 cloves garlic, minced
2 tablespoons cilantro, minced
1 teaspoon freshly ground black pepper
8 swordfish steaks (1/2 pound each)
1 recipe Tequila and Sun-Dried Tomato Salsa

In a small bowl, mix the olive oil, garlic, cilantro, and black pepper until well combined. Coat the swordfish steaks generously with this mixture and allow fish to marinate for at least 2 hours.

When ready, grill swordfish over a hot fire, approximately 3 minutes on each side for 1-inch-thick steaks, and serve immediately, topped with Tequila and Sun-Dried Tomato Salsa.

SERVES 8

TEQUILA AND SUN-DRIED TOMATO SALSA

2 tablespoons gold tequila
1 teaspoon canned chipotle chile, puréed
2 tablespoons tomato paste
1/2 teaspoon dried oregano
1/2 teaspoon brown sugar
1/4 cup rice wine vinegar
2 tablespoons sun-dried tomatoes
1/4 cup olive oil

Combine all ingredients except the olive oil in a blender or food processor. While processing, gradually add oil until the salsa is smooth.

MAKES 1 CUP

SEA BASS BAKED IN BANANA LEAVES WITH MARINATED ARTICHOKE SALSA

6 (10- by 10-inch) banana leaf wrappers
6 sea bass fillets (7 ounces each)
1 recipe Marinated Artichoke Salsa

Preheat oven to 350 degrees. For ease of handling, briefly warm the banana leaves directly over a gas stove burner with low flame or in the oven.

With the shiny side of the wrapper facing down, place the sea bass fillet in the center, spread one-sixth of the artichoke salsa (a little more than half a cup) evenly over the fillet, and overlap two sides of the banana leaf by folding toward each other. Fold the other side underneath the bass to form a tight package. Repeat this procedure until each fillet is wrapped.

Place on a cookie sheet and bake for 18–20 minutes. Serve immediately, breaking the banana leaf packages open with a knife at the table.

SERVES 6

MARINATED ARTICHOKE SALSA

2 jars marinated artichokes (6 ounces each),
*   chopped*
½ cup sun-dried tomatoes, chopped
½ cup cured black olives, pitted and chopped
½ cup cilantro, chopped
2 cloves garlic, minced
¼ cup olive oil
½ teaspoon freshly ground black pepper

In a small bowl, mix all the ingredients until combined well. Use at room temperature. When refrigerated, salsa keeps well for up to 3 days.

MAKES 3½ CUPS

Before there was tinfoil, or even parchment paper, people wrapped food in all kinds of natural wrappers to help retain and enhance flavors. If you can't get banana leaves, try for avocado or ti leaves. If all else fails, go ahead and use parchment paper, a brown paper bag, or tinfoil. This dish is simple to prepare and gets everyone's attention whenever it's served.

Rather than calling for fresh artichokes, which are wonderful to behold but time consuming to prepare, I've made the recipe for the salsa in which the bass is baked easy for all those who prefer to simply pick out their favorite brand of marinated artichokes at the market. Use the salsa not only as a cooking partner in baked foods as we do in this dish but as a topping for almost any grilled food.

HERB-CRUSTED SEA BASS WITH STEWED GOLDEN TOMATO SALSA

Take advantage of this recipe when summer tomatoes are at their peak and fresh herbs are plentiful. (If fresh herbs are not available, use dried herbs and reduce the quantities listed by half.) I will substitute golden tomatoes in almost any recipe calling for red tomatoes. The sweet, low-acidic quality of these tomatoes provides a dramatic change in flavor when used in place of the red. Golden tomatoes are particularly interesting in marinara sauce! This salsa is also an excellent accompaniment with chicken and other mild-flavored fish.

¼ cup peanut oil
6 sea bass fillets (7 ounces each)
2 tablespoons fresh basil, chopped
2 tablespoons fresh chives, chopped
1 tablespoon fresh tarragon, chopped
2 cloves shallot, chopped
2 tablespoons coarse salt
1 teaspoon freshly ground black pepper
1 recipe Stewed Golden Tomato Salsa

Oil the fish fillets lightly and sprinkle the fresh herbs over them evenly. Season with salt and pepper, grill over hot coals for 3–4 minutes on each side, depending on thickness of fillets, and serve on a pool of Stewed Golden Tomato Salsa.

SERVES 6

STEWED GOLDEN TOMATO SALSA

3 tablespoons olive oil
4 cloves garlic, minced
2 cloves shallot, minced
1 cup Spanish onion, sliced thinly
2 tablespoons fresh basil, chopped
1 tablespoon fresh thyme, chopped
1 tablespoon fresh tarragon, chopped
8 large yellow tomatoes, halved and seeded
½ cup chicken stock
½ cup balsamic vinegar
1 tablespoon coarse salt
½ teaspoon freshly ground black pepper

In a saucepan, heat the oil over moderate heat and sauté the garlic, shallot, and onion until translucent. Add the fresh herbs and cook for 1 minute. Then, add the tomatoes, stock, and vinegar and continue cooking for 10–15 minutes, until tomatoes turn into pulp. Season with salt and pepper. Serve warm.

MAKES 3 CUPS

GRILLED SEA BASS WITH LEMON BARBEQUE BASTE

LEMON BARBEQUE BASTE

⅔ cup fresh lemon juice
2 tablespoons fresh thyme, chopped
2 tablespoons fresh chive, chopped
2 tablespoons Worcestershire sauce
2 tablespoons honey
3 cloves shallot, minced
¼ cup olive oil
1 teaspoon freshly ground black pepper

¼ cup peanut oil
6 sea bass fillets (7 ounces each)
2 tablespoons coarse salt
1 teaspoon freshly ground black pepper

To make the baste, mix together the lemon juice with the chopped herbs, Worcestershire sauce, honey, and shallot in a bowl. Whisk in the olive oil. Season with black pepper. Allow flavors to develop for half an hour before using. This baste can be made 2–3 days in advance. If not used shortly after making, refrigerate.

Oil the fish fillets lightly and season with salt and pepper. Grill over hot coals for 3–4 minutes on each side, depending on thickness. Baste frequently. Baste one last time just before removing from the grill.

SERVES 6

For those of you who enjoy a simple piece of grilled fish with a squeeze of fresh lemon, this one's for you.

The Lemon Barbeque Baste originated with the idea of creating a true Californian sauce. It should come as no surprise that tomato products are not used, that it should be used to baste foods rather than as a sauce, and that it doesn't go very well with ribs, unless you happen to have access to ribs from a 150-pound sea bass. The baste is healthy and tastes great with mild seafood and chicken. What would you expect from California?

SHRIMP WITH
THREE-TOMATO CHILE

Why does chile have to cook a long time? I wanted to change the concept of chile into something that has a fresh quality and can be quick. This recipe is what I came up with. The nice thing about this method of cooking chile is that the flavors remain distinct, which makes eating much more enjoyable. You can feature all sorts of ingredients other than shrimp, such as swordfish, scallops, chicken, and beef tenderloin.

4 tablespoons (½ stick) sweet butter
2 cloves garlic, minced
1½ pounds shrimp, peeled and deveined
  (see directions on page xix)
½ cup red bell pepper, julienned
½ cup Anaheim chile, seeded and julienned
  (see directions on page xix)
1 tablespoon ground cumin
¼ cup chile powder
¼ teaspoon dried oregano
¼ cup cilantro, chopped
1 cup tomatillos, diced
½ cup sun-dried tomatoes, diced
1 cup yellow tomatoes, diced
½ cup white wine
1 tablespoon coarse salt
¼ teaspoon freshly ground black pepper

In a large skillet over high heat, melt the butter. Add garlic and stir while cooking for 30 seconds; add the shrimp and continue to stir while cooking for another minute. Put in the pepper, chile, spices, and herbs and cook for 1 minute; then, add the tomatillos, sun-dried tomatoes, yellow tomatoes, and white wine and cook over high heat until mixture thickens. Season with salt and pepper and serve.

SERVES 4

BLT—Bacon, Linguini, and Tomato (recipe on page 75) and ⇒
Chinese Chicken Ravioli (recipe on page 76)

*Overleaf: Grilled Beef Tenderloin with Red Pepper Rajas and
Blue Cheese (recipe on page 123)*

GRILLED SHRIMP WITH CUCUMBER AND TOASTED SESAME SALSA

¼ cup peanut oil
2 tablespoons cilantro, minced
1 tablespoon Teriyaki Sauce (page 7)
1 teaspoon fresh lemon juice
24 large shrimp, peeled and deveined
    (see directions on page xix)
1 recipe Cucumber and Toasted Sesame Salsa

Combine peanut oil, cilantro, Teriyaki Sauce, and lemon juice. Place shrimp on 4 skewers and marinate the shrimp in this mixture for half an hour before grilling.

When ready to grill, cook shrimp over hot coals for approximately 1½–2 minutes on each side, so they are just cooked through at the thickest part, and serve on a bed of Cucumber and Toasted Sesame Salsa.

SERVES 4

CUCUMBER AND TOASTED SESAME SALSA

¾ cup cucumber, peeled, seeded, and diced
¼ cup tomatoes, peeled, seeded, and diced
    (see directions on page xviii)
2 tablespoons white sesame seeds, toasted
    (see directions on page xviii)
1 tablespoon fresh chive, chopped
¼ cup rice wine vinegar
2 tablespoons tomato paste
1 teaspoon garlic and chile paste
2 teaspoons Teriyaki Sauce (page 7)
1 teaspoon sesame oil

In a small bowl, combine the cucumber, tomatoes, toasted sesame seeds, and chive. In another bowl, mix the remaining ingredients briefly, until combined. Pour the liquid mixture over the cucumber mixture and chill. Serve the same day it is prepared.

MAKES 1½ CUPS

This combination is great as a light salad entrée. I created the salsa to challenge myself. For years I had neglected the cucumber for no special reason. I wasn't about to put it in a salad, that's nothing new. In this salsa, the cucumber stars, adding a refreshing touch to the popular flavor of toasted sesame seeds. We also serve this salsa with fresh, grilled Hawaiian Ahi, and it's great with chicken.

Take care not to overmarinate the shrimp as the Teriyaki Sauce will become overwhelming and the lemon juice will cook them before they ever get on the grill.

GRILLED JUMBO PRAWNS WITH CABBAGE AND MAUI ONION CREAM

At rare times, we can get fresh prawns caught about 12 miles off the San Diego coast. They're so sweet and succulent, I actually prefer them to lobster.

The recipe specifies peeling and deveining the shrimp, but if you don't mind the bother of removing prawns from their shells after they're cooked, cook them with shells on as they retain more flavor and moisture.

¼ cup peanut oil
3 cloves garlic, minced
¼ teaspoon freshly ground black pepper
2 teaspoons fresh lime juice
⅛ teaspoon crushed dried red chiles
16 jumbo prawns, peeled and deveined
*   (see directions on page xix)*
3 cups Napa cabbage, sliced thinly
1 recipe Maui Onion Cream (page 12)

Combine peanut oil, garlic, pepper, lime juice, and chiles. Skewer prawns on 4 skewers and marinate them for half an hour in this mixture.

When ready to grill, place prawns over hot coals for approximately 1½–2 minutes on each side, so they are just cooked through at the thickest part.

To serve, place a bed of Napa cabbage nestlike on the plate, place prawns inside, and ladle hot Maui Onion Cream over all.

SERVES 4

LOBSTER "CHOW MAINE"

6 cups coarse salt
5-gallon pot boiling water
4 live Maine lobsters (1¼ pounds each)
1½ cups (3 sticks) sweet butter, barely melted

Add salt to the pot of boiling water; when water returns to a boil, plunge the live lobsters in and cook over the highest heat your stove can provide for exactly 6 minutes. Remove from the water immediately. Carefully, split the lobsters in half, lengthwise, with a knife; crack claws with a hammer; and serve with sweet butter.

SERVES 4

As far as I'm concerned, there's no better way to eat lobster than the way it's prepared in Maine: simply boiled in salty sea water and dipped in sweet butter. This recipe will help you out if you don't have access to sea water and will give you guidelines for cooking lobster to the proper state of deliciousness.

TORTILLA-CRUSTED CHICKEN WITH MEXICAN BEER SALSA

This is about as elegant a chicken taco as you're going to find. I just turned the taco inside out. Instead of filling a tortilla with chicken, I simply broke the tortilla into pieces and wrapped them around the chicken.

2 small eggs
1 tablespoon water
2 cups fresh corn tortillas, coarsely processed
4 chicken breasts, skinless and boneless
        (6 ounces each)
½ cup flour
¼ cup peanut oil
1 cup Mexican Beer Salsa (page 4)

Combine the eggs and water in a small bowl, mixing with a fork until combined. Chop the tortillas roughly and place in a food processor. Process until they resemble coarse bread crumbs.

Dredge chicken breasts, skinned side only, first through the flour, then the egg mixture, and finally press firmly into the tortilla crumbs so they adhere.

Heat a skillet over moderate heat and add the oil. Sauté the crust side of the chicken for approximately 2 minutes, until it is golden brown. Then, turn chicken breasts and cook for an additional 2–3 minutes. Serve on a pool of Mexican Beer Salsa.

SERVES 4

GRILLED CHICKEN
WITH SWEET CORN SALSA

2 cloves garlic, minced
2 tablespoons fresh lime juice
1 teaspoon chile powder
½ teaspoon freshly ground black pepper
2 tablespoons coarse salt
¼ cup peanut oil
4 chicken breasts, boneless (6 ounces each)
1 recipe Sweet Corn Salsa (page 14)

Combine the garlic, lime juice, chile powder, pepper, and salt with the peanut oil. Marinate chicken breasts in this mixture 2 hours before grilling.

When ready, grill chicken over hot coals, 3–4 minutes on each side, until done. Serve on a bed of Sweet Corn Salsa.

SERVES 4

When we first put this on our menu, people marveled at how good it was. They even ordered the salsa separately so they could take it home. Then we gave out the recipe and people marveled at how easy it was. Another case of carefully selecting a few popular ingredients and putting them together to make something yummy.

GRILLED CHICKEN
WITH SPICED MELON SALSA

In Thailand, the origin of this
salsa recipe, it is served as a re-
freshingly spiced fruit salad.
As a salsa, it makes a wonderful partner for grilled shrimp
and chicken. If spice isn't always nice, go ahead and moderate, or even eliminate, the
use of crushed chiles. The
combination of flavors provided by the fruit and vinegar will
supply plenty of wonderful
sensations.

Serve this dish when you want
something light, or something
easy, something you can have
on your diet, and something
that's healthy.

¼ cup peanut oil
2 cloves shallot, minced
2 tablespoons fresh lime juice
1 tablespoon honey
4 chicken breasts, skinless and boneless
    (6 ounces each)
2 tablespoons coarse salt
¼ teaspoon fresh ground pepper
1 recipe Spiced Melon Salsa

Mix together the peanut oil, shallot, lime juice, and honey
until well combined. Marinate chicken breasts in this mixture for
2 hours.

When ready to grill, remove chicken from the marinade, season with salt and pepper, and place over hot coals for 3–4 minutes
on each side. Serve topped with Spiced Melon Salsa.

SERVES 4

SPICED MELON SALSA

¾ cup watermelon, diced
½ cup honeydew melon, diced
½ cup cantaloupe, diced
½ cup cilantro, chopped
½ cup seasoned rice wine vinegar
4 tablespoons sugar
½ teaspoon crushed dried red chiles

Combine all ingredients in a small bowl and mix gently until
integrated. Best served chilled on the same day it is prepared.

MAKES 2¾ CUPS

CHICKEN BREAST WITH GOAT CHEESE AND SUN-DRIED TOMATO SALSA

4 chicken breasts, boneless (6 ounces each)
6 ounces goat cheese (such as Montrachet)
1 tablespoon coarse salt
½ teaspoon freshly ground black pepper
2 tablespoons olive oil
1 recipe Sun-Dried Tomato Salsa

Place chicken breasts skin side down on the counter. Divide goat cheese among the 4 breasts and spread the cheese in the center of each breast, leaving ½-inch border from the edge. Fold each breast over to enclose the cheese and season with salt and pepper.

Warm the olive oil in a large skillet over moderate heat; when heated, place chicken in the skillet and cook until golden brown, approximately 4–5 minutes on each side. Remove from skillet and serve with a large dollop of room-temperature Sun-Dried Tomato Salsa.

SERVES 4

Maybe our style of eating *has* strayed from stuffed chicken breast dishes, but this one is so easy. Living in California, there was absolutely no way I could avoid combining sun-dried tomatoes and goat cheese in at least one recipe!

Sun-dried Tomato Salsa is definitely haute, not hot. The intense flavors of the dried tomatoes are wonderfully complemented by the balsamic vinegar. This salsa is versatile enough to be used on meats and seafood as well as poultry and is quite good tossed with fresh pasta.

SUN-DRIED TOMATO SALSA

¾ cup sun-dried tomatoes, diced
¼ cup cilantro, chopped
1 clove garlic, minced
1½ tablespoons balsamic vinegar
2 tablespoons olive oil
⅛ teaspoon coarse salt
⅛ teaspoon freshly ground black pepper

In a small bowl, combine the sun-dried tomatoes, cilantro, garlic, and balsamic vinegar. Whisk in the olive oil. Season with salt and pepper. Serve at room temperature. Refrigerated, keeps well for 1 week.

MAKES 1 CUP

MEXICAN BARBEQUED RABBIT WITH PINEAPPLE SALSA

1 pound achiote paste
3 cups orange juice
2 rabbits, cleaned and cut into pieces
1 recipe Pineapple Salsa (page 6)

I took a lot of grief when I first put rabbit on the menu at Pacifica Grill. So it happened to be Easter Sunday! No matter what anyone tells you, rabbit doesn't taste like chicken, it tastes like rabbit. It's good, it's healthy, and it's plentiful.

Crumble the achiote paste into the orange juice and stir until completely dissolved. Marinate the rabbit in this mixture overnight.

When ready to grill, remove rabbit from marinade and grill slowly over low to moderate heat, turning the meat from time to time, for approximately 12–15 minutes. Serve with Pineapple Salsa.

SERVES 4

CANARDITAS

6 large duck thighs and legs
6 tablespoons coarse salt
1½ teaspoons fresh ground black pepper
1 quart (4 cups) rendered duck fat or peanut oil
8 cloves garlic
2 tablespoons black peppercorns
½ cup duck or chicken stock

FIXIN'S
12 (10-inch) flour tortillas, warmed
1½ cups sour cream
1½ cups Fresh Tomato Salsa (page 2)
1½ cups Avocado Salsa (page 2)
1½ cups Red Onion and Orange Salsa (page 6)

Season duck thighs and legs with salt and pepper. In a large kettle, heat duck fat with the garlic and black peppercorns over extremely low heat; when fat is warm, immerse the duck in it and cook over low heat for 2 hours, or until the duck is very tender and about to fall away from the bone. Remove duck from the fat and allow to cool. When duck is cool enough to handle, remove the skin and bones and tear the meat into thin strips.

When ready to serve, reheat meat in a pan with the stock and drain before placing it on a plate. Serve family style with the Fixin's.

SERVES 4

This dish rolled around in my head for years before I was able to put it on the menu at Pacifica Grill. The base recipe for the duck is a French confit, similar to what we prepared at the Quilted Giraffe in New York City, and one of my all-time favorites. My dilemma: how to sneak this French dish onto a Mexican and Southwest-influenced menu.

While I realized the cooking technique was similar to the method for making *carnitas*, a well-known regional Mexican pork dish, it wasn't until I mentioned this to my wife Crystal and she quipped, "what are you going to call it, *canarditas?*" that my dilemma was solved. The combination of the word "carnitas" and the French word for duck, *canard*, was all I needed.

CHINESE BARBEQUED DUCK, SCALLOPS, AND VEGETABLES WITH TAMARIND STIR-FRY SAUCE

This dish, one of the more involved recipes in the cookbook (though not really difficult), is definitely worth making. Prepared in the same style as Chinese Barbeque pork, it's a treat for those who have an aversion to pork.

The stir-fry sauce is a great change of pace from the usual heavy soy sauce varieties. Tamarind paste, available in Asian and Indian specialty markets, adds a wonderful tart citrus quality that I balance with the sweetness of mirin, the cooking wine of Japan. You'll also want to use this sauce as a glaze for ham and grilled chicken.

2 cups hoisin sauce
½ cup dry sherry
¾ cup soy sauce
6 duck thighs
3 tablespoons peanut oil
1½ pounds sea scallops, skewered
1½ cups red onion, sliced ¼-inch thick
2 cups broccoli florets
2 cups carrot, peeled and sliced
1 cup red bell pepper, julienned
1 cup fresh baby corn, cleaned
1 recipe Tamarind Stir-Fry Sauce

In a small bowl, mix together the hoisin sauce, sherry, and soy sauce until blended. Reserve half of the mixture; with the other half, marinate the duck thighs overnight.

Preheat oven to 375 degrees. Place the duck on a rack in a roasting pan with water in the bottom pan that does not rise above the level of the rack. Cover pan and place in the oven; cook for approximately 2 hours, until the duck is fork tender. It may be necessary to add more water from time to time to maintain the water level for steaming.

When duck is tender, remove the pan's cover, increase the oven temperature to 425 degrees, and with the reserved marinade, baste the thighs every 5 minutes for about 20 minutes until a crisp glaze is formed. Remove duck from the oven and keep warm.

Place a large skillet or wok over high heat, add the peanut oil; when hot, add the scallops and stir while cooking for 1 minute. Continuing to stir, quickly add the vegetables and cook another minute. Add the Tamarind Stir-Fry Sauce. Cover skillet and steam for 1–2 minutes, until the vegetables are done to your liking. Position a duck thigh in the center of each plate, surround with the vegetables and scallops, and serve immediately.

SERVES 6

TAMARIND STIR-FRY SAUCE

1 cup mirin
1 cup Teriyaki Sauce (page 7)
2 tablespoons tamarind paste
2 tablespoons cornstarch
2 tablespoons cold water

In a small saucepan over moderate heat, combine and bring mirin, Teriyaki Sauce, and tamarind paste to a boil.

Dissolve cornstarch in the cold water and whisk into the saucepan. Bring the mixture back to a boil and remove the saucepan from the heat immediately. Refrigerated, this sauce keeps well for weeks.

MAKES 2¼ CUPS

SMOKED DUCK WITH SMOKY BARBEQUE SALSA

This dish uses my not-so-famous barbeque sauce. If, however, you think it is as good as I do, you can send letters to national food companies and suggest they contact me for the rights. The key is to use the smokiest bacon available. You can, however, eliminate the bacon and substitute a teaspoon of Liquid Smoke, which you can find hanging out near the ketchup in most supermarkets.

You'll need to use your smoker to prepare this dish.

2 ducklings (5 pounds each), washed
½ cup coarse salt
2 tablespoons freshly ground black pepper
½ cup brown sugar
1 recipe Smoky Barbeque Salsa
1 recipe Sweet Corn Salsa (page 14)

Wash and clean the ducklings, then pat dry. Cut the ducks into individual pieces: thigh and leg as one piece, breast and wing the other piece.

Combine the salt, pepper, and brown sugar in a small bowl. Season duck well with this mixture.

Place duck on a rack in your smoker; smoke over very low heat, 225 degrees, for 1 hour. After that time, baste duck with Smoky Barbeque Salsa every 15 minutes for the next hour, or until the meat is tender. At that point, raise heat in smoker (or, if need be, your oven) to 400 degrees and baste duck every 5 minutes for about 20 minutes, until a nice glaze forms. Serve on a bed of Sweet Corn Salsa.

SERVES 4

SMOKY BARBEQUE SALSA

1/4 pound smoked bacon, diced
1/2 cup red onion, diced
2 cloves garlic, minced
3/4 teaspoon cayenne pepper
2 teaspoons ground cumin
2 small jalapeño peppers, seeded and diced
       (see directions on page xix)
1 teaspoon freshly ground black pepper
1 teaspoon dried oregano
2 cups chicken stock or water
2 cups ketchup
1/4 cup cilantro, chopped
1/4 cup dark brown sugar
2 tablespoons Worcestershire sauce
1 teaspoon Tabasco sauce
1 tablespoon fresh lemon juice

In a saucepan, cook the diced bacon until it begins to crisp. Add the onion and garlic to the bacon and its rendered grease and stir while cooking for 2–3 minutes. Add the cayenne, cumin, jalapeño, black pepper, and oregano and cook for another minute. Add the remaining ingredients, bring to a simmer, and continue cooking, uncovered, over low heat for 30 minutes. Serve warm. Salsa keeps well for 1 week when refrigerated.

MAKES 4 CUPS

GRILLED LEG OF LAMB WITH CILANTRO PESTO

It's been my experience that people are either "lamb people" or they're not. I've also found that people who have tried lamb and say they don't like it because they find it gamy probably didn't eat lamb raised in this country.

We get the restaurant's lamb from Colorado, and it's surprising how many have changed their minds about liking lamb.

This straightforward recipe, great for large groups, is even better for small groups because you can enjoy the leftovers.

1 leg of lamb (4–5 pounds), boneless and
    butterflied
1 cup olive oil
12 cloves garlic, minced
1 bunch cilantro, chopped
1 teaspoon freshly ground black pepper
1 recipe Cilantro Pesto (page 19)

Marinate the lamb in a mixture of olive oil, garlic, cilantro, and black pepper for 24 hours before cooking.

When ready to grill, place chops over hot coals and, turning frequently, cook for approximately 7–9 minutes total on each side for medium rare. Remove from grill and allow to rest 10–15 minutes before slicing. Serve with Cilantro Pesto on the side.

SERVES 8–10

GRILLED LAMB CHOPS WITH JALAPEÑO MINT JELLY

8 double rack lamb chops, trimmed
¾ cup olive oil
6 cloves garlic, minced
3 tablespoons fresh rosemary, chopped
2 tablespoons fresh thyme, chopped
3 tablespoons fresh basil, chopped
2 teaspoons freshly ground black pepper
1 recipe Jalapeño Mint Jelly

Marinate lamb chops in a mixture of olive oil, garlic, the fresh herbs, and black pepper for 24 hours before cooking.

When ready to grill, place lamb chops over hot coals, cooking approximately 3–4 minutes on each side for medium rare. Serve with Jalapeño Mint Jelly on the side.

SERVES 4

I can think of no better meat entrée than lamb that has been enhanced with a marinade of fresh herbs and lots of garlic.

The homemade jelly that accompanies the lamb is intentionally on the loose side to give it more appeal as a sauce or glaze than its counterpart on the supermarket shelf. For those of you who think jalapeño jelly is weird, wait till you try it with peanut butter!

JALAPEÑO MINT JELLY

1 large Anaheim chile, seeded and diced
    (see directions on page xix)
4 jalapeño peppers, seeded and diced
    (see directions on page xix)
1 tablespoon fresh mint, chopped
2½ cups sugar
¾ cup rice wine vinegar
2 tablespoons water
½ packet (about 1 ounce) powdered fruit pectin

Combine chile, peppers, and mint with sugar in a food processor or blender and process for about 2 minutes, until the chiles are pulverized. Transfer mixture to a saucepan that contains the remaining ingredients, bring to a boil, and simmer 3 minutes. Strain, being sure to press the solids well to extract all the flavor. Chill before serving.

MAKES 2¼ CUPS

GRILLED VEAL CHOPS WITH PEANUT SAUCE

A good veal chop doesn't need much to make it great. Add the Peanut Sauce, with Asian and Mexican influences, and enjoy veal at its best.

PEANUT SAUCE

1 tablespoon sweet butter
2 cloves garlic, minced
1 small jalapeño pepper, seeded and minced
       (see directions on page xix)
¼ cup light soy sauce
½ cup cream of coconut
½ cup water
1 cup chunky peanut butter
1 bunch cilantro, chopped

4 rack veal chops (¾ pound each)
2 tablespoons peanut oil
2 tablespoons coarse salt
½ teaspoon freshly ground black pepper

For the Peanut Sauce, warm butter in a small saucepan over moderate heat; add the garlic and minced jalapeño and continue cooking for 1 minute. Add soy sauce, cream of coconut, water, peanut butter, and cilantro and stir until sauce is smooth. Simmer over low heat for 10 minutes. Keep sauce warm.

Coat veal chops with peanut oil and season with salt and pepper. Grill over hot coals, approximately 3 minutes on each side for a 1-inch-thick chop, until veal is medium rare. Serve with a generous ladle of Peanut Sauce spooned over the top.

SERVES 4

FILLET AND SCALLOPS WITH ORIENTAL MUSTARD SALSA

3 tablespoons peanut oil
2 cloves garlic, minced
¾ pound beef tenderloin, cut into cubes the size
*   of sea scallops*
¾ pound sea scallops
2 large red bell peppers, cut into long strips
24 asparagus spears (3 inches each)
¼ cup dry vermouth
1 recipe Oriental Mustard Salsa (page 9)

In a large skillet or wok over high heat, heat peanut oil until it begins to smoke. Carefully, add garlic and the cubed beef, stirring until browned on all sides. Add the sea scallops and continue to cook, stirring occasionally, for 2 minutes; then, add the peppers and the asparagus spears and cook for 1 minute more. Pour in the vermouth, allowing it to reduce in the pan until almost no liquid remains. Last, add the Oriental Mustard Salsa, stir to coat all ingredients, and serve.

SERVES 4

Surf and turf needn't always be steak and lobster. Searing the scallops in the same pan as the beef adds a wonderful flavor to this dish. Bathed in Oriental Mustard Salsa, my version of an Oriental steak diane sauce, this dish makes stir-fry elegant.

BRAISED VEAL SHANKS
WITH HOT AND SOUR SAUCE

It's been established that Italians brought pasta to Italy from China, and there is speculation that Italians may have discovered pesto there, as well. Is it possible that China could have originated osso buco?

½ cup peanut oil
6 veal shanks (1 pound each)
12 cloves garlic
2 cups onion, diced
2 cups mushroom caps, whole
1 teaspoon dried tarragon
4 cups tomatoes, diced
2 cups balsamic vinegar
2 tablespoons green peppercorns
1 cup Teriyaki Sauce (page 7)
2 cups water
½ cup mirin
2 tablespoons chile and garlic paste
2 tablespoons brown sugar
1 tablespoon sesame oil

Preheat oven to 350 degrees. In a large skillet over high heat, heat half the peanut oil until it begins to smoke and sear veal shanks until they are brown on all sides. Remove shanks from the pan and set aside.

Lower heat to moderate and add the remaining peanut oil. When hot, put in the garlic, onion, mushroom caps, and tarragon and cook, while stirring, until the onion is translucent. Add the tomatoes, vinegar, and green peppercorns and cook until the liquid is reduced by half. Add the Teriyaki Sauce, water, mirin, chile and garlic paste, and brown sugar; bring mixture to a boil.

Return veal shanks to the skillet, cover, place in oven, and cook until the meat is fork tender, approximately 1½ hours. Skim any fat that accumulated on the surface of the braising sauce, add the sesame oil, and serve.

SERVES 6

GRILLED BEEF STEAK MARINATED IN BEER

6 rib eye steaks (10 ounces each)
6 cloves garlic, minced
1 tablespoon freshly ground black pepper
1 bottle (12 ounces) dark beer or ale
2 tablespoons coarse salt

Rub each steak with garlic; then, season with the black pepper. Lay steaks in a single layer in a large dish. Pour beer over the steaks. Refrigerate, allowing steaks to marinate overnight; turn them once in the process.

When ready to grill, remove steaks from the marinade, season with salt, and place over hot coals until they are done to your preference (2–3 minutes on each side for a 1-inch-thick steak is medium rare).

SERVES 6

Beer tenderizes and adds flavor to beef. Although I specify rib eye, which I believe is one of the most savory cuts for this purpose, you can substitute a sirloin, New York strip, or any cut of steak that you prefer. Escalloped Tortillas (recipe on page 131) is a great sidekick for this dish.

GRILLED BEEF STEAK
WITH TWO-PEPPER SALSA

This pepper steak, which leans toward the French rather than the Chinese version of pepper steaks, exhibits its own unique flavor, provided by the capers and tarragon vinegar in the Two-Pepper Salsa.

The salsa is a variation of a sauce that was created at Lavin's Restaurant in New York City where I worked as dinner chef. Great on red meats! If you really love peppers, you may want to add jalapeño peppers to the salsa as well.

6 cloves garlic, minced
2 tablespoons coarse ground black pepper
1/2 cup olive oil
6 rib eye steaks (10 ounces each)
2 tablespoons coarse salt
1 recipe Two-Pepper Salsa

Combine garlic and black pepper with the olive oil and marinate the steaks in this mixture overnight, or at least 2 hours before grilling.

When ready to grill, season the steaks with salt. Cook over hot coals, approximately 2–3 minutes on each side for a 1-inch-thick steak to obtain medium rare. Top each steak with a generous amount of Two-Pepper Salsa and serve.

SERVES 6

TWO-PEPPER SALSA

2 large red bell peppers, diced small
1/3 cup capers, minced
1/4 cup green peppercorns, minced
1 clove garlic, minced
2 tablespoons tarragon vinegar
1/4 cup olive oil
3 tablespoons parsley, chopped
1/2 teaspoon coarse salt
1/8 teaspoon freshly ground black pepper

In a bowl, combine red bell peppers with the capers, peppercorns, and garlic. Add the tarragon vinegar and whisk in olive oil. Add chopped parsley and season with salt and pepper. Serve at room temperature. This salsa is best when used the same day it is prepared.

MAKES 3 CUPS

GRILLED BEEF TENDERLOIN WITH RED PEPPER RAJAS AND BLUE CHEESE

4 cloves garlic, minced
1 tablespoon coarse ground black pepper
¼ cup cilantro, chopped
¼ teaspoon crushed dried red chiles
¼ cup olive oil
4 beef tenderloin steaks (6 ounces each)
4 tablespoons (½ stick) sweet butter, room
*   temperature*
2 ounces blue cheese, room temperature
2 large red bell peppers
2 tablespoons coarse salt

Beef tenderloin earned its reputation for tenderness, not flavor, so I always like to pair tenderloin with stronger partners. Here, the tenderloin is enhanced with roasted pepper strips and blue cheese.

Combine the garlic, black pepper, cilantro, red chiles, and olive oil and marinate the steaks in this mixture for at least 2 hours before cooking. Put butter and blue cheese in a bowl and mix until thoroughly integrated. Set aside until ready to serve.

Turning frequently on a hot grill, cook the red bell peppers until the skins are charred. Set aside and allow to cool to room temperature. When cool enough to handle, peel, seed, and cut the peppers into strips ¼-inch wide. Set aside until ready to serve.

When ready to grill the steaks, season them with salt and cook over hot coals until they are done to your taste. To serve, place steaks on plates and top each with red pepper strips and a generous tablespoon of the blue cheese butter.

SERVES 4

GLAZED PORK CHOPS WITH PAPAYA AND SWEET PEPPER SALSA

ANCHO-HONEY GLAZE
6 tablespoons honey
1 tablespoon Red Chile Paste (page 5)
½ tablespoon fresh lime juice

2 tablespoons peanut oil
6 pork chops (¾ pound each)
2 tablespoons coarse salt
½ teaspoon freshly ground black pepper
1 recipe Papaya and Sweet Pepper Salsa

To make the glaze, place ingredients in a bowl and mix until combined. Refrigerated, keeps 2–3 months, so you can make this well in advance. Use at room temperature.

Oil the pork chops lightly and season with salt and pepper. Grill over hot coals until done, approximately 3–4 minutes on each side. Just before removing pork chops from the grill, brush generously with Ancho-Honey Glaze. Serve the chops, topped with Papaya and Sweet Pepper Salsa.

SERVES 6

Pork chops and sweet glazes are no strangers. This glaze adds some spice but is cooled by the Papaya and Sweet Pepper Salsa. Use papaya that's ripe and sweet. Take the opportunity to treat yourself to this salsa often—it's good with almost everything, especially smoked meats.

Don't believe the rumor that pork must be cooked all the way through to prevent serious health complications. Raising pork has become a fine art, so leave some moisture in those chops to see how wonderful they can be.

PAPAYA AND SWEET PEPPER SALSA

1 medium papaya, peeled, seeded, and diced
1 medium red bell pepper, diced
1 medium yellow bell pepper, diced
1 clove garlic, minced
3 tablespoons cilantro, chopped
2 tablespoons fresh lime juice
1 tablespoon honey
½ cup olive oil
⅛ teaspoon coarse salt
1 pinch freshly ground black pepper

In a bowl, mix together the papaya, peppers, garlic, cilantro, lime juice, and honey. Carefully stir in the olive oil. Season with salt and black pepper. This salsa is best when served at room temperature the same day it is prepared.

MAKES 3 CUPS

SIDEKICKS

One of the ways I judge the food at other restaurants is by the treatment of the vegetables and starches that accompany entrées. Too often, restaurants place secondary importance on these dishes and, more often than not, this lack of attention carries over to their star attraction.

Sidekicks should be true companions. Although they are meant to enhance the entrée, they should be treated to an equal amount of consideration during preparation. You'll often find, as we do, that sidekicks garner as much praise and appreciation as the main course. The following recipes are a case in point.

BASIC BLACK BEANS

We use this recipe as a base for preparing our Southwestern Black Bean Soup and Baja Baked Beans, but it's also satisfying as "just good old black beans" over rice. The epazote is not essential but does ease the gaseous effect that beans are known to produce.

1½ cups dried black beans
3 tablespoons epazote or *1 bunch fresh cilantro,*
*   chopped*
1 tablespoon ground cumin
1 tablespoon chile powder
3 cloves garlic, minced
2 teaspoons dried oregano
½ cup onion, diced
6 tablespoons tomato paste
2 tablespoons coarse salt
¼ teaspoon freshly ground black pepper

Soak the black beans overnight in 6 cups of cold water. Drain. In a large saucepan, combine the beans with all remaining ingredients. Add enough water to cover ingredients, place over low heat, bring mixture to a boil, and simmer gently until beans are tender, approximately 45 minutes to an hour.

SERVES 4

BAJA BAKED BEANS

I once wondered for a moment whether Boston had cornered the market on baked beans. I concocted this recipe just to prove it wasn't true.

4 cups Basic Black Beans, with juices
1 tablespoon canned chipotle chiles, puréed
1 cup brown sugar
1 can (6 ounces) tomato paste
¼ cup red wine vinegar

Preheat oven to 350 degrees. In a bowl, combine all ingredients. Place in a casserole dish and put in the oven. Bake until the top begins to dry and get crusty, approximately 45 minutes to 1 hour. Serve hot.

SERVES 6

JICAMA-PEANUT SLAW

DRESSING

2 cups mayonnaise
6 tablespoons white wine vinegar
3 tablespoons dry mustard
¾ cup sugar
¼ cup red onion, minced
1 tablespoon white pepper
½ cup peanut butter

SLAW

6 cups jicama, peeled and shredded
2 large red bell peppers, julienned
1 bunch fresh cilantro, chopped
½ cup golden raisins
1 cup roasted peanuts

For the dressing, place all ingredients in a large bowl and mix until combined.

To make the slaw, combine all ingredients, toss with the dressing, and serve.

SERVES 6

I created this dish rather than to try to compete with our patrons' favorite family coleslaw recipes. By simply replacing cabbage with jicama, a sweet root vegetable, and adding all-American peanut butter to a creamy slaw dressing, I ended up with this most delicious result, which we've been serving as a sidekick to our signature Mustard Catfish for years.

CURRIED RICE PILAF

One of the most difficult tasks in a professional kitchen is teaching the art of seasoning to unseasoned cooks. Until your teaching takes hold, your task is to come up with a foolproof method to assure "good taste" when you're not around. This rice, using Teriyaki Sauce as a preseasoned stock, was created with that goal in mind.

3 tablespoons sweet butter
¾ cup onion, diced
3 cloves garlic, minced
1½ tablespoons curry powder
1¼ cups long-grained rice
½ cup Teriyaki Sauce (page 7)
1¾ cups water
½ cup jicama, peeled and diced small
½ cup carrots, diced small
¼ cup currants
1 bunch cilantro, chopped

Melt the butter in a skillet or saucepan over moderate heat; then, add the onion and garlic and cook until onion is translucent. Add the curry powder and rice and stir until the rice is coated by butter. Pour in the Teriyaki Sauce and water, bring to a boil, cover, reduce heat to low, and simmer gently for approximately 14 minutes, until all liquid is absorbed. Stir in the remaining ingredients and serve immediately.

SERVES 4–6

ESCALLOPED TORTILLAS

2 tablespoons sweet butter
1 cup onion, sliced thinly
3 cloves garlic, minced
½ cup flour
4 cups milk
1¼ cups freshly grated Parmesan Cheese
1 tablespoon coarse salt
½ teaspoon freshly ground black pepper
6 ounces crisp tortilla chips, unsalted

This recipe has its roots in regional Mexican cuisine. It's a great alternative to escalloped potatoes and a marvelous way to use those tortilla chips that went stale when you forgot to seal the bag.

Preheat oven to 350 degrees. Melt butter in a saucepan over moderate heat, add the onion and garlic, and cook until the onion is translucent. Stir in the flour until all the moisture is absorbed; then, stir in the milk, 1 cup of the Parmesan cheese, salt, and pepper. Bring the mixture to a boil, add the tortilla chips, and simmer until tortillas become soft.

Remove from heat and pour mixture into a casserole dish. Sprinkle the remaining ¼ cup of cheese over the top and place casserole in the oven. Bake until the top begins to brown, approximately 30 minutes, and serve.

SERVES 6–8

CREAMY POLENTA

4 cups water
2 tablespoons coarse salt
1 teaspoon freshly ground black pepper
3 tablespoons sweet butter
½ cup sun-dried tomatoes, diced
½ cup scallions, sliced thinly
2 cups cornmeal
1 cup heavy cream

Combine everything, except the cornmeal and heavy cream, in a saucepan and bring mixture to a rolling boil. Whisk in the cornmeal gradually while stirring constantly. Lower heat and continue to stir for 2 minutes. Mix in the cream, cook another minute, and serve.

SERVES 6

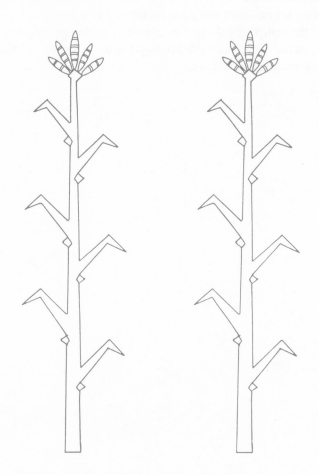

SPINACH AND WILD RICE PANCAKES

2 cups spinach, cooked
¾ cup wild rice, cooked
¼ cup onion, diced small
2 cloves garlic, minced
1½ tablespoons coarse salt
½ teaspoon freshly ground black pepper
¾ cup bread crumbs, toasted (see directions
*   on page xviii)*
4 eggs
3 tablespoons sweet butter

Spinach should be cooked, squeezed dry, and chopped before measuring. In a bowl, combine the spinach with the wild rice, onion, garlic, salt, pepper, bread crumbs, and eggs. Form the mixture into 12 pancakes.

Melt butter in a skillet over moderate heat and fry pancakes until they are brown, approximately 2 minutes on each side. Serve warm.

SERVES 6

When my grandmother was getting on in years and her eyesight was failing, she insisted on making her famous cheesecake for us. We swallowed, smiled, and never told her she had accidentally put cream cheese with chives in the cheesecake. And, somehow, we never got around to asking grandmother for the recipe. I did, however, ask her to teach me how to make these wonderful spinach pancakes, the only recipe I learned from her. Unlike the pancakes you normally serve for breakfast, you'll want to serve these to accompany your dinner entrée, or as a light appetizer or lunch entrée, topped with a dollop of sour cream.

JICAMA HASH BROWNS

When working with new and
unfamiliar ingredients, I'll
often test them by steaming,
baking, frying, grilling, and
sautéing them to observe what
occurs and how I might, or
might not, want to use them.
Such a trial with jicama pro-
duced the seed for these offbeat
hash browns.

3 cups jicama, peeled and shredded
2 cloves garlic, minced
¼ cup onion, diced small
1 tablespoon coarse salt
½ teaspoon freshly ground black pepper
1 teaspoon chile powder
2 tablespoons fresh lime juice
½ cup red bell pepper, diced small
1 bunch cilantro, chopped
¼ cup dry bread crumbs
2 eggs
3 tablespoons sweet butter

Combine all ingredients in a bowl and mix until well combined. Divide mixture into 12 portions and compress into tight,
flat patties.

Preheat a skillet or griddle, melt the butter, and fry hash
browns over moderate heat until they are golden brown on both
sides.

SERVES 6

RED PEPPER RAJAS

Translated, *rajas* is simply
"strips." Although rajas are
Mexican, the pickling liquid I
use is inspired by Asian cooking, creating less heat and
more sweet.

2 cups rice wine vinegar
1 tablespoon whole black peppercorns
1 bay leaf
1 teaspoon crushed dried red chiles
1 teaspoon whole mustard seeds
1 cup sugar
½ cup water
3 large red bell peppers, cut into ½-inch strips

Combine all ingredients except red peppers in a saucepan.
Bring mixture to a boil and simmer for 10 minutes. Remove from
heat and pour over the pepper strips. Allow rajas to chill before
serving.

SERVES 6

GARLIC SMASHED POTATOES

1½ pounds baking potatoes
5 cloves garlic
3 tablespoons coarse salt
¼ cup olive oil
1 teaspoon freshly ground black pepper

Wash the potatoes, leaving skins on, and cut each potato into eight pieces. Place potato in a saucepan with the garlic cloves and 2 tablespoons of the salt and cover with water. Bring water to a boil and simmer until the potatoes are cooked through, approximately 10 minutes. Remove from heat, drain potatoes and garlic, and place in a large bowl.

Mix potatoes and garlic with a beater, adding the olive oil, the remaining tablespoon of salt, and black pepper. Mixture will be lumpy, and the garlic cloves should remain whole. Serve hot.

SERVES 4

Olive oil replaces both butter and cream in this version of mashed potatoes, which has health as well as a wonderful garlicky flavor in mind.

Overleaf: Clockwise from top: Mexican Chocolate Sundae with Kahlua Peanut Sauce (recipe on page 152), The Burnt Cream (recipe on page 142), Chan's Cookies (recipe on page 148)

⇐ *Neil Stuart*

NEW POTATO SALAD

Food can't get much simpler or tastier than this potato salad. People are often disappointed when they ask for the recipe and receive the list of ingredients, thinking it's just another chef's plot to sabotage the home cook by leaving out the secret ingredient.

2 pounds small red new potatoes
2 tablespoons coarse salt
1 cup mayonnaise
½ cup red onion, diced
1 bunch cilantro, chopped
¼ cup pine nuts, toasted (see directions on
*   page xviii)*
½ teaspoon freshly ground black pepper

Wash the potatoes, leaving skins on, quarter them, place in a saucepan with 1 tablespoon of the salt, and cover with water. Bring water to a boil and simmer until the potatoes are cooked through, approximately 10 minutes.

Remove from heat, drain potatoes, and chill. When potatoes are cold, mix with the remaining ingredients and serve.

SERVES 4–6

SPICY ROAST POTATOES

If you manage to have any of these left over, try crisping them in oil and serving as chile fries.

2 pounds small red new potatoes
¼ cup olive oil
2½ tablespoons coarse salt
5 tablespoons Spanish paprika
½ cup chile powder

Preheat oven to 350 degrees. Wash the potatoes and dry with a towel. Coat the whole potatoes lightly with olive oil. Mix spices together; then, roll the potatoes in the spices to completely coat. Place potatoes on a pan and roast them in the oven until tender, approximately 45 minutes. Serve hot.

SERVES 4–6

POTATO, CHILE, AND SWEET CORN HASH

½ pound baking potatoes
½ cup fresh corn kernels
1 red bell pepper, diced small
1 Anaheim chile, seeded and diced small
    (see directions on page xix)
¼ cup scallions, sliced thinly
1 tablespoon coarse salt
½ teaspoon freshly ground black pepper
3 tablespoons sweet butter

Wash and julienne the potatoes finely, leaving skins on, as if making matchstick potatoes. Wrap potato in a towel and squeeze out all the excess moisture that you can. In a bowl, toss the julienned potato with the corn kernels, diced pepper, scallions, and salt and pepper.

Melt butter in a skillet over moderate heat and place small piles of the potato mixture in the pan as if making pancakes, taking care not to compress the mixture so hash will remain light. Cook until the hash reaches a rich golden brown, approximately 2 minutes on each side. Remove from pan, drain on a paper towel, and serve.

SERVES 4

Hash browns are usually considered breakfast food. By squeezing out the excess moisture and starch, we make these potatoes so incredibly light and elegant that they'll fit right in with the most formal of dinners. Serve this as a sidekick to a hearty steak or grilled chicken dish. You might even want to eat it as an appetizer topped with Fresh Tomato Salsa (recipe on page 2).

FINAL TEMPTATIONS

The satisfaction of making your own desserts will be exceeded only by the satisfaction of eating them. When I was head chef at the 23rd Street Bar and Grill, I found myself at odds with the owner, Stanley Bernstein, as to whether we would purchase our desserts or prepare them in-house. I, of course, wanted to make our own. Stanley acceded to my wishes under the condition that I teach the dishwasher to prepare the desserts. Little did I know that the dishwasher could neither read nor write. Little did Stanley know that this man was so intelligent and eager to take on the challenge that he was able to memorize and execute the recipes perfectly. The dishwasher moved up to the position of sous-chef.

One word of precaution that should be noted when baking is that weight measurements are far more precise than volume measurements, particularly for dry ingredients such as flour. Where I've included both methods, you should use the weight specification if you have a scale available.

KAHLUA POACHED PEARS

This is one of those "change of pace" desserts that is so surprisingly good that people come back and order it again and again. The basis for this recipe was provided by Steve Pickell, one of our former chefs. It's delicious, too, accompanied with a healthy scoop of coffee ice cream.

6 pears
8 cups freshly brewed coffee
1½ cups Kahlua liqueur
1 cup fresh orange juice
2 tablespoons fresh lime juice
1½ cups sugar
2 cinnamon sticks

First, peel the pears; then, slice the bottom edge with a knife so pears will stand upright. With a melon baller, carefully scoop from the bottom end of the pear until the entire core is removed.

Place pears in a large saucepan with the remaining ingredients, making sure they are fully covered by liquid (placing a small towel on top of the pears to keep them submerged may be necessary). Over low heat, cook the pears until they are fork tender. Carefully remove them from the liquid so they can cool.

Meanwhile, remove cinnamon sticks from the liquid, increase heat to high, and boil liquid down until it begins to turn into a syrup. Remove from heat and put in the refrigerator to cool.

When ready to serve, spoon syrup over the cold pears.

SERVES 6

KONA CHOCOLATE LAVA TORTE WITH SWEET COCONUT CREAM

15 tablespoons (almost 2 sticks) sweet butter,
   room temperature
4 ounces bittersweet chocolate
1½ ounces unsweetened chocolate
½ cup powdered sugar
1 tablespoon coffee extract
1 teaspoon vanilla
3 eggs
½ cup flour
2 tablespoons cocoa
¾ teaspoon baking powder
1 recipe Sweet Coconut Cream

Lightly grease six 1-cup soufflé dishes with 3 tablespoons of the butter. Over a double boiler, melt the chocolates; then, add the remaining butter and the powdered sugar, stirring until dissolved. Transfer mixture to a bowl; add the coffee and vanilla extracts, the eggs, flour, cocoa, and baking powder; and beat with a mixer until it becomes mousselike. Divide the mixture between the greased soufflé dishes, cover, and freeze.

When ready to bake, preheat oven to 375 degrees. Place the frozen cups directly into the hot oven and bake for 10–13 minutes, until the edges are set but the center retains a moist appearance. Remove from the oven and allow tortes to rest for 10–15 minutes; invert tortes on a plate and serve with Sweet Coconut Cream.

SERVES 6

I named this dessert "lava" torte so I wouldn't have to explain that the runny center was intentional and not a problem of underbaking. You can prepare the torte three to four weeks in advance and freeze it until ready to serve, so it's the perfect dessert when you want the convenience of making something ahead of time, as well as having it come fresh out of the oven shortly before serving.

SWEET COCONUT CREAM

1 can (14 ounces) coconut milk
2 tablespoons brown sugar

Combine coconut milk and brown sugar in a saucepan and cook over moderate heat until mixture reduces to 1 cup, approximately 10 minutes. Remove from heat. Chill before serving.

MAKES 1 CUP

THE BURNT CREAM

6 egg yolks
¾ cup sugar
1 tablespoon vanilla
3 cups heavy cream
½ cup milk
6 tablespoons brown sugar

Preheat oven to 350 degrees. In a bowl, mix the egg yolks, sugar, and vanilla. Set aside. In a saucepan over moderate heat, combine the cream and milk and bring to a full boil; then, while stirring, slowly pour into the egg yolk mixture. Divide among six 6-ounce baking cups, place in a deep baking pan with water half way up the baking cups, and bake for approximately 40 minutes, or until the custard is set in the center. Remove from the oven and allow custard cups to cool at room temperature; then, refrigerate until needed.

When ready to serve, preheat broiler. Spread a thin, even layer of brown sugar over the top of the custard. Place under the broiler to caramelize the brown sugar to a light brown. Wait a few minutes for the sugar to cool before serving.

SERVES 6

CHOCOLATE-CINNAMON TORTE

CHOCOLATE MOUSSE

12 ounces bittersweet chocolate
12 eggs, separated
¾ cup sugar
1 teaspoon vanilla extract
1 teaspoon coffee extract

CINNAMON BUTTERCREAM

4 tablespoons (½ stick) sweet butter, room
  temperature
2 teaspoons ground cinnamon
1 egg white
3 tablespoons sugar
½ cup heavy cream

DECORATION

2 cups chocolate shavings

Most chocolate desserts are "death by sugar." Not true of this dessert. You should, however, expect to feel strongly sedated when you partake of this pleasurable light chocolate creation.

Preheat oven to 350 degrees. Butter and flour one 10-inch springform pan.

For the mousse, melt chocolate over a double boiler. Whip the 12 egg yolks and the sugar with a mixer until light. Fold the melted chocolate, vanilla, and coffee extracts into the egg yolk mixture. Whip the 12 egg whites with mixer until they reach a soft peak; fold egg whites into chocolate. Divide the mixture in two, placing one half in the refrigerator to set and the other half in the springform pan. Bake the mixture in the springform pan for 10–13 minutes, until set. Remove from oven and allow to cool.

To make the buttercream, melt the butter half way; then, with a whisk, whip butter until it has a consistency like mayo. Whip in the ground cinnamon. In a separate bowl, whip the egg white and the sugar to a soft peak; fold into the cinnamon butter. Finally, whip the cream to a soft peak and fold that into the cinnamon mixture.

To assemble the torte, spread the cinnamon buttercream evenly over the cooled baked mousse. Then, spread the refrigerated mousse over the cinnamon buttercream. Top with chocolate shavings. Refrigerate and allow to set for 2 hours before serving.

MAKES A 10-INCH TORTE

CHEESECAKE IN A GLASS

This dessert holds two memories for me: the memory of cheesecake, though it is clearly lighter and there is no cheese in it, and the memory of my first taste of French food at Robaire's Restaurant in Los Angeles, when I was thirteen years old. I had coq au vin, and I loved it. The reason for the latter memory is that this dessert is from Robaire's, which, after an extremely long run, recently closed its doors.

4 egg yolks
¼ cup plus 2 tablespoons sugar
3 tablespoons fresh lemon juice
1 teaspoon lemon zest
1¼ cups sour cream
½ cup yogurt
2½ cups heavy cream
2 tablespoons sugar

In a mixing bowl, combine the egg yolks with ¼ cup of the sugar and the lemon juice and zest. With a whisk, whip the mixture over a double boiler continuously, until it thickens and increases in volume like whipped cream. Remove from heat and allow to cool to room temperature.

Mix the sour cream and yogurt together and fold into the cooled egg mixture. Whip the cream and the remaining 2 tablespoons sugar to a soft peak and fold into the sour cream mixture. Put in stemware and chill for 2 hours before serving.

SERVES 6

LEMON-TEQUILA MOUSSE

2½ cups heavy cream
⅔ cup superfine sugar
4 medium lemons, juice only
2 tablespoons gold tequila

Combine all ingredients and beat with a mixer until the cream attains a soft peak. Remove mousse to a serving container and chill for 2 hours before serving.

SERVES 4

Superfine sugar, or quick-dissolving bar sugar, is essential to this recipe. Look for it in the market where they sell alcoholic drink mixes. That in hand, this recipe is as simple as whipping cream. If tequila is not to your taste, leave it out, and make it a lemon mousse.

WHITE CHOCOLATE AND TOASTED HAZELNUT MOUSSE

6 ounces white chocolate
¼ cup milk, warmed
¼ Frangelico liqueur
¼ cup hazelnuts, toasted and chopped finely
     (see directions on page xviii)
2 egg whites
2 tablespoons sugar
1 cup heavy cream

In a double boiler, melt the white chocolate slowly. Remove from heat and stir in the warmed milk, Frangelico, and the toasted hazelnuts. Allow this mixture to cool to room temperature.

In a mixer, whip the egg whites, while adding the sugar gradually, to a soft peak. Fold egg whites into the cooled white chocolate mixture. Last, whip the heavy cream to a soft peak and fold this into the white chocolate mixture. To allow mousse to set, put in a serving dish to cool at least 2 hours before serving.

SERVES 4

My very first week as a student at the Culinary Institute of America, William Grant and Company sponsored a student recipe contest to help introduce Frangelico liqueur. Unshaken by my rookie status, I entered and six months later was judged the winner for this very mousse.

BAKED APPLE TARTS
WITH CARAMEL–MACADAMIA
NUT SAUCE

Preparing individually por-
tioned desserts is incredibly
time consuming, but the results are usually elegant. This
recipe provides a time-saving
approach to creating miniature
apple tarts that you can bake
quickly and serve warm. When
you add Caramel–Macadamia
Nut Sauce and vanilla ice
cream, how could you go
wrong?

6 (4-inch) frozen puff pastry rounds
2 tablespoons sweet butter, room temperature
¼ cup sugar
3 medium baking apples
1 recipe Caramel–Macadamia Nut Sauce
6 small scoops vanilla ice cream

Defrost puff pastry in the refrigerator overnight. Preheat oven
to 425 degrees. Butter 6 flat-bottomed 1-cup baking cups, and
sprinkle buttered surfaces with sugar. Peel, core, and cut each apple into 8 equal wedges. Arrange half an apple, or 4 wedges, in
each cup as if the half were still 1 piece (with the flat side of the
half against the bottom of the cup). Top each cup with puff pastry,
place cups on a cookie sheet, and bake until the pastry is golden
brown, about 20 minutes. Remove from oven and allow the tarts
to rest for 10–15 minutes.

When ready to serve, invert the tart onto a plate and remove
cup, top with Caramel–Macadamia Nut Sauce, and finish with a
scoop of vanilla ice cream. Serve immediately.

SERVES 6

CARAMEL—MACADAMIA NUT SAUCE

1 cup sugar
2 cups heavy cream
2 tablespoons sweet butter
1 tablespoon honey
1 teaspoon vanilla
1 tablespoon maple syrup
½ cup macadamia nuts, toasted and chopped
    (see directions on page xviii)

In a heavy saucepan over moderate heat, combine sugar with 1 cup of the heavy cream, the butter, and honey. Stirring occasionally, bring mixture to a boil; continue to stir while mixture boils until it turns a light golden brown. Remove from heat and stir in the remaining cup of cream, the vanilla, maple syrup, and macadamia nuts. Allow sauce to cool to room temperature before using.

MAKES 2 CUPS

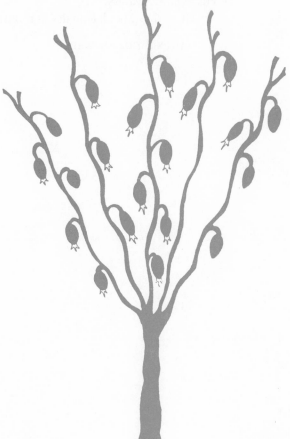

CHAN'S COOKIES

I get a certain amount of plea-
sure when I use ingredients for
purposes other than those for
which they were intended. I'll
go out of my way to challenge
myself. These cookies were
created by such a challenge.
The flavor of wonton skins is so
neutral, you'll want to keep the
ingredient that makes these
wafers so light a mystery. Let
the Charlie Chans of the world
try to figure out your secret.

1 cup peanut oil
24 wonton skins
4 ounces bittersweet chocolate, melted
4 ounces white chocolate, melted
½ cup sesame seeds, toasted (see directions on
page xviii)

Heat peanut oil in a skillet over moderate heat. When hot, fry
the wonton skins, trying to keep them flat, until they are a light
golden brown. Remove and drain the cooked wafers on paper towels. Repeat until all the skins are cooked.

Next, lay the wafers flat on a cookie sheet. Using a fork, drizzle the dark chocolate over one side of the wafers in an irregular
pattern until all the chocolate is used. Repeat procedure with
white chocolate. While chocolate is still wet, sprinkle sesame
seeds over the wafers.

Allow the chocolate to dry at room temperature and serve.

MAKES 2 DOZEN WAFERS

COCONUT–CHOCOLATE CHIP COOKIES

¾ cup (6 ounces) vegetable shortening
¾ cup (6 ounces) sugar
2 large eggs
1 teaspoon almond extract
2 cups (6 ounces) sweetened shredded coconut
1½ cups (6 ounces) flour
6 ounces chocolate chips

Preheat oven to 350 degrees. In a mixer, beat shortening and sugar until well combined. Continuing to mix, add the eggs and almond extract; when combined, add coconut. Then add the flour, mixing only until it is incorporated. Stir in the chocolate chips.

Drop cookie dough by the tablespoon on a greased and floured cookie sheet, making sure to slightly flatten the top of each cookie. Bake for about 20 minutes, or until the edges just begin to turn a light brown color. Cool before serving.

MAKES 3 DOZEN COOKIES

One of my early jobs was pastry chef of Clever Hans Bakery in Ithaca, New York. In this small European-style bakery, much of the work was done by hand. I still have vivid memories of making upwards of five hundred pounds of cookies a week, all dropped by hand on baking pans. Even with this memory, I still like to make these cookies, which were, hands down, the most popular of the bunch.

TOASTED PECAN
BUTTER COOKIES

This is a nutty version of the classic French butter cookie. It's my favorite to sit down and eat with a warm cup of hot chocolate.

12 tablespoons (1½ sticks) sweet butter, cold
1½ cups (6 ounces) flour
¼ cup (1 ounce) pecans, toasted and ground
*   finely (see directions on page xviii)*
¾ cup plus 1 tablespoon (6¼ ounces) sugar
2 tablespoons cold water
1 egg white

Cut the butter into small pieces; in a food processor, combine it with the flour, pecans, and ¼ cup plus 1 tablespoon (or 2¼ ounces) of the sugar. Process until the mixture resembles a fine meal. Continue to process while adding the water. When mixture begins to come together, remove from the processor and form it into a log, 1½ inches in diameter, and wrap with plastic wrap. Chill or freeze the log until ready to bake.

Preheat oven to 350 degrees. Remove cookie log from plastic wrap and brush it with the egg white. Roll log in the remaining sugar and cut into round cookies that are ¼-inch thick. Place cookies on a baking sheet and bake until they take on a light brown color, about 15–18 minutes. Remove cookies from the oven and cool before serving.

MAKES 3 DOZEN COOKIES

LEMON TART WITH
FRESH BLUEBERRIES

¾ cup (1½ sticks) sweet butter, cold
⅔ cup powdered sugar
1½ cups flour
1 pinch salt
4 eggs
1½ cups sugar
¼ cup fresh lemon juice
1 teaspoon fresh lemon zest
2 cups fresh blueberries
1 cup heavy cream, whipped

This quick and easy lemon tart recipe, good in its own right, is deserving of fresh blueberries when you can get them in season.

Preheat oven to 350 degrees. Cut the butter into small pieces and place in a food processor along with the powdered sugar, flour, and salt. Process until the mixture takes on the appearance of coarse sand. Turn mixture out onto a 10-inch tart pan, spread evenly, and press onto pan to form a crust. Place pan in oven and bake until crust begins to appear dry, about 20–25 minutes.

Mix the eggs, sugar, lemon juice, and zest together and pour into the tart crust after it has reached the dry stage. Continue baking for another 20 minutes or so until the filling has set. Remove pan from the oven and allow tart to cool to room temperature. Serve tart topped with blueberries and whipped cream.

MAKES A 10-INCH TART

MEXICAN CHOCOLATE SUNDAE WITH KAHLUA PEANUT SAUCE

Everyone appreciates it when you go out of your way to bake a special dessert. But give them an ice cream sundae and watch their appreciation turn into smiles. Sometimes it's easier than you think to please people.

1 flour tortilla
1 cup peanut oil
¼ cup powdered sugar
1 quart dark chocolate ice cream
1 recipe Kahlua Peanut Sauce
1 cup heavy cream, whipped
⅓ cup unsalted peanuts, chopped

Cut flour tortilla into 6 wedges. Heat peanut oil in a skillet over moderate heat; when hot, fry the tortilla wedges until crisp and drain on a paper towel. When dry, sprinkle wedges thoroughly with powdered sugar.

To assemble the sundaes, place the ice cream in cups, top first with Kahlua Peanut Sauce, then the whipped cream, and finally the chopped peanuts. Garnish with the fried tortillas.

SERVES 6

KAHLUA PEANUT SAUCE

6 ounces bittersweet chocolate
½ cup Kahlua liqueur
½ cup water
1 tablespoon sweet butter
½ cup peanut butter

In a double boiler, melt the chocolate and combine with the Kahlua, water, and butter. Remove from heat, add the peanut butter, stirring until incorporated, and serve.

MAKES 2 CUPS

INDEX

Mustard
    about, 17
    catfish, 88
    Chinese hot, 9
    jalapeño honey, 17
    marinade, 88
    Oriental salsa, 9
Mustard Catfish, 88
    sidekick for, 129

N, O
New Potato Salad, 136
No-Bean Chile, 59
Noodles. *See* Pasta
Nuts, toasting, xviii
Oil, xix–xx
Onion(s)
    about, 12
    fritters with pineapple salsa, 35
    quesadilla, potato and, 38
    salsa
        Maui cream, 12
        red onion and orange, 6
Orange salsa
    burnt orange sauce, 53
    red onion and, 6
Orange-and-Ginger-Glazed Lamb Riblets, 51
Organization, importance of, xviii
Oriental fermented black beans
    about, xxiii
    salsa, 8
        lobster cassoulet with, 48
        pasta with, 73
        wok-charred catfish with, 89
Oriental Mustard Salsa, 9
    fillet and scallops with, 119
Oysters, baked with cilantro pesto, 37

P
Pacific Southwest cuisine, xvi
Pacifica Blue Plates, xi
Pacifica Del Mar, xi, 9
Pacifica Grill, xi, 111
Panko bread crumbs, xxiii
Papaya and Sweet Pepper Salsa, 125
    glazed pork chops with, 124–25
Pappardelle, spinach, with sea scallops and jalapeño
        cream, 78

Pasilla chiles, xxi
Pasta, 73–85
    about, 73
    fettuccini, spicy seafood, 84
    linguini
        bacon and tomato, 75
        sweet crab with golden tomato curry sauce and,
            82–83
        wild mushrooms, 74
    pappardelle, spinach, with sea scallops and jalapeño
            cream, 78
    penne, chicken and toasted pecans, 79
    ravioli
        Chinese chicken, 76
        Gorgonzola with sweet red pepper cream, 85
    rigatoni, swordfish with tomato, basil, almond salsa
            and, 80–81
    soba noodles, xxiv
        kung pao calamari with, 77
Pastries. *See* Desserts
Pastry, puff, xxiii
Pastry skins, xxii
Peanut Sauce, 118
    grilled veal chops with, 118
Peanut(s)
    jicama slaw, 129
    Kahlua peanut sauce, 152
    sauce, 118
    spicy vinaigrette, 70
Pears, Kahlua poached, 140
Pecans
    butter cookies, 150
    penne with chicken and, 79
Peeling
    shrimp, xix
    tomatoes, xvii
Penne, chicken and toasted pecans with, 79
Penne with Chicken and Toasted Pecans, 79
Pepper
    black vs. white, xx
    Szechuan peppercorns, xxiv
Peppers (hot). *See* Chiles
Peppers (sweet)
    chicken quesadilla, roasted red pepper and, 40
    red pepper rajas, 134
        grilled chicken with blue cheese vinaigrette and, 71
        grilled tenderloin with blue cheese and, 123
    roasting, xix

THE BEST OF RESTAURANT COOKING

by Mark Miller

"Mark Miller's Coyote Cafe in Santa Fe, in both its design and dishes, is bold and exciting. And his book is all of those qualities combined."—*Washington Post*

Exciting, innovative Southwestern cuisine, from the nationally known restaurant.

Full color throughout. $24.95 clothbound, 160 pages

by Janos Wilder

"A splendid and creative assortment of 200 recipes . . . a graceful mix of simplicity and elegance."—*Booklist*

Recipes and tales from a celebrated Tucson restaurant which mixes classic French cookery with the vibrant tastes of the Southwest.

Full color photographs. $24.95 clothbound, 228 pages

by Keo Sananikone

" . . . filled with uncomplicated recipes and photographs that manage to be useful and beautiful at the same time."
—*Chicago Tribune*

Keo's Thai restaurant is one of *the* places to visit in Hawaii, and the wonderful recipes in this book prove that its reputation is definitely deserved.

Full color throughout. $21.95 clothbound, 192 pages

by Margaret Fox and John Bear

Food from a beautiful little restaurant in Northern California which celebrates fresh ingredients, great food, and country living. Also, hints and stories for anyone considering starting a restaurant.

$14.95 paper or $19.95 cloth, 224 pages

MORNING FOOD

by Margaret Fox and John Bear

Fabulous breakfast, brunch, and light lunch recipes from the widely known and loved Cafe Beaujolais include everything from the expected eggs, coffee cakes, and muffins to the unusual, such as a breakfast burrito, pasta, and salads.

$19.95 clothbound, 208 pages

THE STREAMLINER DINER COOKBOOK

by Alexandra Rust, Elizabeth Matteson, Judith Weinstock, and Irene Clark

Diner food as you've never had it before from a small cafe near Seattle which has gained a great reputation for honest, fresh, made-from-scratch American food.

$19.95 clothbound, 192 pages

BAYSWATER BRASSERIE BOOK OF FOOD

by Tony Pappas and Hamish Keith

Casual, hearty food from one of the best and most popular restaurants in Australia—the Bayswater Brasserie in Sydney. Recipes for breakfast, lunch, dinner, light suppers, and picnics.

Full color illustrations. $24.95 clothbound, 192 pages

Ten Speed Press
Box 7123
Berkeley, CA 94707
(510) 845-8414

Available from your local bookstore, or order direct from the publisher. Please include $1.25 shipping & handling for the first book, and 50 cents for each additional book. California residents include local sales tax. Write for our free complete catalog of over 400 books and tapes.